Call Me Jobulene

A Story of Courage and Determination

Vera Simpson Gaines

Copyright © 2025 by Vera Simpson Gaines

ISBN: 979-8-88615-222-7 (Paperback)
979-8-88615-285-2 (Hardback)
979-8-88615-286-9 (Ebook)

All rights reserved. No part of this publication may be reproduced, distributed, or transmitted in any form or by any means, including photocopying, recording, or other electronic or mechanical methods, without the prior written permission of the publisher, except in the case brief quotations embodied in critical reviews and other noncommercial uses permitted by copyright law.

The views expressed in this book are solely those of the author and do not necessarily reflect the views of the publisher, and the publisher hereby disclaims any responsibility for them.

Inks and Bindings
888-290-5218
www.inksandbindings.com
orders@inksandbindings.com

Contents

Dedication: v

Chapter 1
The Early Years 2

Chapter 2
Tragedy Strikes 9

Chapter 3
Salvation 17

Chapter 4
Abandonment 20

Chapter 5
Independence 27

Chapter 6
Marriage 30

Chapter 7
Children 37

Chapter 8
Lies And Deceptions 44

Chapter 9
    Health Problems..53

Chapter 10
    Back Against The Wall..72

Chapter 11
    Prayers To God..75

Chapter 12
    Charity...78

Chapter 13
    Coming Out Of The Storm..83

Chapter 14
    Lessons Learned 86

Chapter 15
    Planting Seeds 89

Chapter 16
    Making Yourself Available 92

Chapter 17
    Why Am I Here?..95

DEDICATION:

I have to first dedicate this book to the Lord Almighty because without Him, I would not be here today. Second, I give my precious mother in heaven credit for raising me in a Christian home and teaching me at an early age that nothing is more important than God. She taught me that we are passing through this place, and our real home is in heaven with God and Jesus Christ. Third, I have to give my husband Gary credit for putting up with me over the years when it hasn't been easy. Fourth, I have to thank my daughters Heather and Tiffany for helping me with the editing and artwork, but most of all for making my life worth living when I wanted to throw in the towel.

CHAPTER 1

THE EARLY YEARS

I was born on April 9, 1949, the fifth of five children to Raymond and Clara Powell Trussell Simpson. I was the only child in the family to be born in Houston, Mississippi. My father was a soil conservationist, and the family moved a lot. Not only did my father have an eight-to-four job, we also had a dairy and a farm to tend to. This meant that everybody had to help to get everything done.

Being the last child my parents would have, I was spoiled and not expected to do a lot in the way of work. I still hear about how spoiled I was, and I will be the first to admit that, yes, I was spoiled rotten. Babies tend to be spoiled. I learned at an early age to use my golden ringlets and big blue eyes to get me things and attention that I thought I needed. To make matters worse, I was the last of nine grandchildren on my father's side and the next to last on my mother's side.

The Birth Order Book is one of the most enlightening books I have ever read. This book explained to me why I felt I was not worth much to the family. With four older siblings, most in the upper range of intelligence, and the fact that just about everything I could ever think about doing had already been done, that didn't leave much for me. I feared I would never measure up to the greatest expectations of me coming from a talented and gifted family.

Mother kept telling me to be my own person and not to follow the crowd. I remember once she asked me, "If everyone were to jump off a cliff, would you jump too?" I thought that was the stupidest thing I had ever heard her say. Saying stupid things was not my mother's style. She was extremely gifted. She went off to Blue Mountain College at the tender age of fifteen. She was on the swim team and played the violin in the orchestra. She also was in the drama club, which sometimes took her on the road. I guess if she had been one to follow instead of lead, she wouldn't have been at college at that age. I remember her telling me she wasn't accepted by many because of her age. It didn't slow her down, and I guess that's good because her time here on earth was very short. I've learned it's not the year that you were born or the year that you die that's so important---it's what you do with the dash. Her dash was filled with a lifetime of friends, joy, happiness, goals, and also trials and tribulations. Mother filled her fifty years with all that the Lord needed her to do. I was only sixteen when I buried my mother, and I didn't understand at that time why God needed her more than me. I was angry with God for a very long time.

To make matters worse, I was the only child left at home, and I didn't have a good relationship with my father. I realized that my father had fallen in love with one of my mother's nurses, who was married, before my mother died. My heart was broken into so many pieces. I would scream out at God, asking Him over and over, "Why are you doing this to me?" I thought He must have been punishing me for something.

Things went from bad to worse when my father made me break a date to drive him to see Mary in another town two weeks after my mother's funeral. Mary's husband had left the day mother died, going to California to see one of their daughters for a month. You have never heard anything so sickening in all your life as two old people carrying on in the kitchen while I sat in the living room with her oldest daughter. I think if either one of us had had access to a gun, we would both be in prison for murder. I couldn't even grieve properly for my mother with all this mess going on. To make the story short, they married as soon as Mary's divorce was final, which was in about six months. I was put in the hospital for exhaustion and stress. I was not going to attend the wedding, but my oldest sister C.P insisted that I attend. I cried through the whole service. My life turned upside down when Mary moved into the house and took over. Suddenly all of the rules changed, and nothing was the same. I felt like I had gone to Hell and couldn't find my way back.

Never in my wildest dreams did I ever think that my life or my dad's would be in danger until one night while we were eating supper. I heard the doorbell ring, and I answered the door. There, to my surprise, stood Mary's ex-husband. I spoke to him, and he was acting very strange. My father called to me from the kitchen, asking who was at the door. I didn't want to tell him. As I turned to answer him in hopes that he would stay in the kitchen, Mary's ex-husband came in the house, and it wasn't until that moment when I turned back around that I saw the gun in his hand for the first time. By now my father had entered the room with Mary right behind him. Mary's ex-husband was drunk and raised the gun to shoot my father with me standing in the direct line of fire. Needless to say, I froze. My father instructed me to call the sheriff, but I didn't want to move for fear Mary's ex-husband would shoot my father at close range. At that distance, I knew he wouldn't miss, drunk or not. I was ordered a second time to call the sheriff, which I did. Talk about looking up a number in a hurry. This was when I needed 911! I was shaking so badly that I didn't know where to look for the number. I think I finally dialed the operator and let her place the call for me. That was the last time I saw Mary's ex-husband. I felt so sorry for him. This was only the beginning of a long nightmare.

I nee to back up a little here to mention another defining moment in my life that would alter my opinion of men forever. It's amazing how the brain protects young children from abuse until a time the brain thinks the person can handle what happened in the earlier years. It was a hot summer day, and I had decided to ride around the farm with my older brother while he was doing chores. Keep in mind this brother was my father's favorite. I was nine years old, and Don was eighteen. He was the brightest and most popular of the family. He graduated at the top of his class and was voted Mr. Houston High School among many other awards. I don't know where his brain was that day, but in my opinion he fell from grace that day. I had placed him on a pedestal and revered him in the highest regard a sister could bestow upon a brother. Without going into too many details, I will say he forced me against my will to do something I'll never forget. Even though I was not physically raped, emotionally I was raped. From that moment on, I could never allow myself to ever be left alone in his presence. If your own brother would do that to you, then what would another man do to you? This was the beginning of a long line of problems for me.

Next, a best friend's grandfather, who followed the basketball teams, would visit people's homes in hopes of finding girls home alone. My mother was at Mississippi State for the summer getting her master's. This left me home alone when my sister decided she needed to go to town to run some errands, and my father was at work. I was thirteen years old and very naïve. I was in the kitchen washing dishes when I heard a knock at the kitchen door. We didn't have a peephole back in those days, so I opened the door not thinking there may be danger behind it. There stood one of the oldest perverts in town, although at the time I didn't have a clue. He asked for my mother, to which I promptly replied that she was at Mississippi State getting her master's, which was mistake number one. He asked to come in, which was mistake number two. I continued to wash dishes, and when I finished I told him he had to leave. When I walked toward him to open the door, he stepped close enough to me to touch my pocket on my shirt, commenting that my pocket was so cute. Give me a break! How many old men notice whether a pocket on a shirt is cute or not? A red flag went up. I demanded he leave immediately, which he did not do, but he tried to continue a conversation. I backed him out onto the back porch, trying to get him outside. At this time, my cousin drove by, and she noticed a strange car in front of the house and that our car was missing. She threw her car in reverse and pulled into the drive. I pushed my way past the old man and started walking toward my cousin, trying to hold back the tears. She could tell he had done something to me, so she demanded that he leave immediately, which he did. Kitty drove me to her house a fourth of a mile down the road, and my father was called home from work. I can visualize that day as clear as if it were yesterday. My father threatened to kill the old man if he ever showed his face again on our property. I never told my best friend, which made it difficult for me, especially when I went home with her because he lived across the road from her. He would see me and would come over. I would lock myself in the bathroom until he left. My best friend still does not know.

My next experience happened at the hospital where I worked for Dr. Dyer. I was instructed to walk an outpatient to the ER to have some stitches taken out. I had no idea this man had been in a lot of trouble even in the waiting room of the hospital. I soon found out to stay clear of this old man. He grabbed me in the hall, and I had to break myself loose from his grip. I took off down the hall with this old man trying his best to keep up with me. I thought my job was over when the operating nurse informed me I had to wait and escort him back to the outpatient department. I waited outside the door, so I could get a good head start. If you could have seen this old man running after me down the hall, you would have laughed yourself silly like the others did. I got a lot of ribbing from this one. Even the doctor told me to stay where he could keep his eye on me. Later I heard how this same man attacked a nurse while she was making calls with one of the doctors, and it took five people to get him off of her! By this time, I'm asking myself why perverts are so attracted to me.

Without boring you any longer, there are several more experiences where I was followed and approached by men. I only wanted to give you some background so you could try to understand why I have not been able to trust men for most of my life, and how it relates to many more problems. All of this plays an important part in my heavenly Father's relationship and how hard it was to believe that He could be trusted when others could not.

My abandonment issues also play an important role in how I have lived in fear of loved ones leaving me. I kept reminding myself of the deal I tried to make with God while my mother lay dying. I wanted God to let me take her place. Take me and let her live because she had so much more to offer the world than I did. But there was also a selfish reason for my asking. I didn't want to be left behind to live without her. I didn't want to live my life in that much pain! If you have never lost a loved one, take my word for it. It's like having your heart dug out with a spoon every minute of the day and night. I didn't have that support system in place at home because Mary didn't want to hear my mother mentioned because she knew how inferior she was to my mother. Mary couldn't hold a light to her, and she knew it. My mother would make Mother Teresa look bad. I thank God as often as possible for allowing me to be born to such a saintly woman. My mother would have given the shirt off her back to anyone who needed it. Thank you Lord, for allowing me to call her "Mother." So many people in this world aren't born to good parents. This is where I am truly blessed!

CHAPTER 2

TRAGEDY STRIKES

My first experience with death came at five years of age, and up until this point I had not lost anyone in my immediate family to death. My first loss was a very dear family friend whom I had considered a father figure. My mother's best friend, Mrs. Inez Castle, was gracious enough to help Mother out by keeping me when Mother decided to go back to work. I was four at the time, and I started out staying up the road with my Aunt Catherine, after whom I'm named, but I think she also went to work shortly around the same time. Since I was so young I barely can remember all the details.

Mrs. Castle took me in when Mother started working full-time at the school instead of part-time. Mother started out part-time as a dance instructor, and I did go with her according to some people who can remember that far back. I do remember dance recitals at the school because I was in some of them. Mother took dance lessons after finishing college, and in just three weeks she had learned enough to start her own dance studio. She mostly taught the lessons at home. Mother taught all of us how to dance; even the boys could tap dance.

Mr. Castle was an important person in my life. He treated me just like all his children. Nancy was a year older than my sister C.P. Tommy was around the same age as our twins Don and John, who were older than their twins Johnny and Judy. My sister Martha

Lou was right behind their twins. Then there was Jennifer, who was six months younger than I was. So our families were very closely integrated in church, school, and social settings. Keep in mind that Houston, Mississippi, was and still is a very small town where everybody knows just about everybody or at least somebody related to someone they know. Not many degrees of separation found there.

Mr. Castle would arrive home in the afternoon before Mother would come to pick me up. Every single day Jennifer and I would watch and wait for J.T. to arrive so we could run out the door and into his arms. He would pick up whoever got there first and throw them up into the air and then reach for the other and do the same. Well, I could run faster than Jennifer, and I was always the first to reach J.T. I took great pride in this until I found out a few years ago how much it affected Jennifer. Then I wished I had been more in tune to the situation and had allowed her to beat me a few times.

One afternoon, J.T crawled under the house to check on some wires, and I can remember it clearly because Jennifer and I squatted down at the opening and watched him disappear into the darkness, never to see him again. We ran off to play, and then Mother came to take me home.

I answered the phone that night after supper only to be told by someone who was very upset that they needed to speak to my mother. I remember hearing my mother scream to my father that J.T. had been found dead under the house. This was so disturbing to me that it started a lot of questions about death. I remember going over to the house, and all the furniture had been moved out of the living room, and the casket was against the wall where the couch usually sat.

Everybody was so distraught, it scared me. I clung to my mother's skirt, and I was so confused about why J.T. was lying in that box and not moving or speaking to anyone. At the graveside Mother kept me at a distance because I was so upset. I can remember everyone crying so loudly, it broke my heart. I was standing there in that graveyard that I asked my mother why everyone was so upset.

She said, "Because they won't get to see their father again until they go to heaven." I didn't know until that day that when a person died that they couldn't come back. This bothered me very much, and I spent a lot of time wondering why. Life isn't like television where a person dies and comes back on another show.

My next experience with death was the burning death of my mother's father. I was in the sixth grade when Grandpa Trussell died. We saw my mother's parents twice a year because they lived on the Gulf Coast, so I didn't know them as well as my father's parents, who lived in the same town with us. A call came in while we were at school; so I didn't get to see my mom before she and my father left in such a hurry, trying to get to the coast before my grandfather died. It was a five to six hour trip, and they didn't get there in time to see him before he passed away.

Grandpa Trussell had magnolia tree on his property that was the largest in the world, and he didn't want anyone to know because he didn't want tourists on his property wanting to see it. He took us down there several times to see it and to swing on a rope from the lowest branch, which was higher than most trees. When we arrived the leaves were so deep they almost engulfed me. While we played, he would rake up the leaves and burn them.

On the day Grandpa Trussell died, the gasoline must have splashed from the can onto his pants without his knowledge as he walked down to the site. When he lit the fire, the fire shot straight up his clothes, burning him over 85 percent of his body. He was in shock. He lived a few hours after arriving at the hospital. It was best that he didn't live being that badly burned. I was not able to attend the funeral since it was so far away. My mother stayed for awhile after the funeral to help Grandmother deal with the loss. Mother didn't talk much when she got home. I didn't know how respected my grandfather was till one day I was working on the family tree and came across his obituary from the paper. I didn't know he was such a fine Christian man until I read statements that others had written about him. I guess I had spent a lot of my time playing with my cousins so that I didn't get to know him like I did my grandmother. I think we all would spend more time with our loved ones if we knew their time was so short. That's why it's so important to me to treat others well and tell them now how much they mean to me while I've got the chance.

The next experience was the most devastating to me, so much so that I almost lost my own life grieving over the loss of my most precious mother. Mother was never sick. She didn't miss church or teaching due to illness until she was diagnosed with cancer. I was eleven years old when Mother, at the age of forty-five, was told she had breast cancer. Surgery was set up as soon as school was out for the summer. I remember getting off the elevator at the hospital and seeing her checked into her room, waiting to have surgery the next morning. I wasn't allowed to be at the hospital while the surgery was taking place. She was home in a short period of time but went off to summer school at Mississippi State to try and pick back up where she left off, working on her master's. Her degree was very important to her. I don't think Grandmother was very happy about Mom going right back to school. I got the impression Grandmother thought she should stay home and take care of herself.

I don't remember the time frame here, but the cancer was not all gone, and she had to go to Jackson, Mississippi, to take cobalt treatments, which she said were very painful. She said she would daydream of me ballet dancing to keep her mind off the pain. I often wondered if Mother had gotten her surgery in Jackson, if she would have had a better chance of beating this disease. We'll never know the answer to that question. The scar was horrible and there was one place that would not heal. There was such a huge hole under the left arm where they had to remove so many lymph nodes. We didn't know then what that means to us today. There were several surgeries and more bad news--- the cancer had gone to the bones. After many lengthy stays in the hospital, Mother decided she wanted to die at home. We honored her request and set up a hospital bed in my bedroom, and I moved into the next room so I would be able to hear her in the night.

I was trained at the age of fourteen to give Mother morphine shots. You would have to know how I hated shots as a child to understand how the health department cringed when they saw me coming. Mother would start weeks in advance preparing me for the shots that were to be required. I couldn't get my summer swimming pass if I didn't get my boosters. The poor health department nurse remembers me well! I pulled away from her during my polio vaccine and kicked her in the shin, and she had to go out in the waiting room and ask a man to come hold me while she re-did my vaccine. So I got stuck twice! I guess that was my payment for being difficult. One time I asked my sister to dig her fingernails into my wrist so I would be distracted while the nurse gave me my shot. However I had gotten immune to my sister's nails because she would use them on me. It would make her so mad when it didn't hurt. After awhile she gave up using them on me.

I trained on an orange or grapefruit to learn how hard to tap the needle against the skin because the skin of the fruit was around the same thickness. Next came the mashing of the pill in the syringe and then adding the sterile water. Then I had to thump the syringe to get all the air bubbles to the top so I could force them out. If you get air into the bloodstream it will kill you. Mother encouraged me along the way because she knew how difficult this task was for me. I had said since I was four years old that I was going to be a nurse because my sisters said they were going to be teachers, and I was going to be sure to be different. Both my mother's parents were teachers. We had a family full of teachers. Remember, Mother told me to be different, not to follow the crowd.

Needless to say, I didn't have a normal childhood because I was forced to perform adult tasks at a very early age and had to sacrifice sleepovers and other events that all my friends were engaged in. I couldn't be gone for long periods of time because I had to be there to give the shots. I also had to get up during the night to massage Mother's feet or ankles due to pressure points or bedsores. Then there were the baths and the enemas. I also spoonfed Mother every meal except when I was in school. During the meals I would update her on all my problems or activities at school. I didn't want her to hear my dad and Mary at the dinner table laughing and carrying on. You could hear through the walls. This enraged me! I knew my father loved my mother dearly, and this was not the same man I saw behaving so poorly. I've always been told "until death do us part" was the way it was supposed to be.

    I know at this point, the morphine was not taking care of all the pain. I asked one day what the pain was like. Mother said it was like a 1, 000 times worse than a toothache. I can't stand just a toothache. I've never forgotten that statement! It has haunted me over and over. Why would God let such a wonderful, sweet, Christian woman suffer for five years in this kind of pain? Mother knew she was going to a better place. She worried about Dad. She knew we would grow up and have families on our own, but she didn't want Dad left alone. If only she knew what was going on right under her nose. I know she would have objected because she wouldn't have wanted Dad to break up another person's marriage at my cost.

    Mother went home to be with the Lord on July 11, 1965 at the tender age of fifty. I was sitting right outside her window in the swing with Aunt Catherine when she left us. She had slipped into a coma a few days before so I didn't get to say goodbye. The next few days were a blur to me. Things were just too difficult for me to deal with. Seeing her in the coffin was one of the hardest things I've ever had to do.

    The church was packed with standing room only. I could not hold my head up. I wanted to run out of the church screaming as loud as I could. I felt like at any moment I would lose control of myself, and I knew Mother would not have wanted that. I tried to be strong for her. God promises never to give us more than we can handle, but this was over the top for me. God was going to have to carry me through this crisis.

Everybody went back to their homes and their towns, and I was left at home alone to deal with the aftermath. I cried myself to sleep every night and spent hours during the day crying till I couldn't cry anymore, and then the anger came. I didn't want anyone giving me any advice or wisdom at this point. I just wanted to die. This is where my first thoughts of suicide came in. I really needed counseling, but no one offered it.

I tried to drown myself in whiskey when I could get my hands on it. We lived in a dry county, so someone had to get it for me. Whiskey may numb you for a short period of time, but you always come to with the same problems you had in the first place. To make matters worse, I started smoking at the same time. I didn't care if I died. To me that was the only way out.

Where was God during all of this? We had conversations on a regular basis, but they were not good conversations. I would vent my anger at him, especially when Mary entered the picture again. I kept hoping I would wake up from this nightmare and it would be just a dream. Unfortunately, Mary came to stay, and I walked out the door when I went off to college. I spent two years at home putting up with this horrible woman, and I could not take anymore. It was six months before I went home for the holidays, and most of the time was spent at friends or in the basement. Mary didn't want me around because I looked just like my mother and I talked like her. I was a constant reminder to my father who he really loved, so I was not treated kindly at all. It didn't do any good to complain to Dad because he would not buck the system. Mary was a holy terror, and he had to live with her. I'm sure my dad paid his dues over and over many times for getting involved with Mary. Everybody suffered from her wrath and guess what? She had a daughter who didn't fall far from the tree. You'll hear about my stepsister later.

CHAPTER 3

SALVATION

All five of us were raised in the church, so we all accepted Jesus Christ as our personal savior at early ages. I walked down the aisle at nine years of age. Everybody who was present for my baptism remembers it well. I had had swimming lessons two summers in a row, so by now I had the breaststroke down real good. If you don't believe me, just ask those who were present that night. Somehow when the preacher brought me back up, my foot slipped off the board they had for us to be able to get out of the baptismal without any difficulty, they thought. When I started going back under, I immediately started swimming out. I had just been saved, and I didn't want to drown in the process! Try to picture me swimming with my feet just kicking up a storm. I can only imagine how wet the preacher must have gotten. My eyes were focused on the steps! The choir director told me later that night that my mother's money was well spent on swimming lessons. I just laughed and skipped on my way. You won't believe this, but I went back to the First Baptist Church for their 150th anniversary, and there are still people alive who remember that night! I'm sure I'll hear something in heaven about it too. I can hear it now!

God blessed me with the most wonderful Sunday school teachers and vacation Bible school teachers I've ever known. I was a whiz at the Bible drills. I took great pride in how fast I could find the verses.

Memory verses were a little harder for me. I had to be moving in order to recite them--- don't ask me why.

I loved filling in the money cards for the Lottie Moon Christmas offering and other missions. I'm sure we've all heard a thousand times at mealtime how there were starving children all over the world, therefore we should clean our plates. I know my mother wasn't the only one saying this. There were times I wanted to pack up my plate and send those starving children the food that was on my plate. I know Mother meant well, but I think this sets people up to overeat. I did not do this to my children.

There is a Bible verse that instructs parents to raise their children in the church, and when they grow old they will not depart from it. I fully believe this. Some of my fondest memories are church related. We could not stay home on Sundays unless we were on our deathbed. If you missed church, you could not go anywhere later in the day, either. I made sure I enforced the same rules in my home.

CHAPTER 4

ABANDONMENT

As much as I wanted to leave home, I think I cried the worst at graduation out of the sixty-three graduates. We were all going different directions. I had signed up to go to Gilfoy Nursing School in Jackson, Mississippi, and no one else in my class had done so. Two weeks before I was to leave for Jackson, I changed my mind and decided to go to Mississippi State along with several others from my class. Quite a few of my friends went off to college and took summer school classes. I wish I had done that. There was nothing to do in such a small town, so most of my time was spent sunbathing and having sleepovers.

Fall finally came and off to college I went. Things seemed so different and exciting in Starkville, Mississippi. I had spent a lot of time there with my family attending games, so it wasn't totally strange to me. It was more like a second home. My brother Don was nuclear engineer in Starkville, so I wasn't alone without someone I could call if I needed help.

I worked almost forty hours a week at the library between classes, at night, and on weekends. It didn't take long to figure out I didn't have good study skills. After a year and a half, I had to make a decision that I needed to be on the other side of the desk or I would be asked to leave like two of my dearest and closest friends. I was not accustomed to making F's. My sister called and threatened to send me to Blue Mountain College if I didn't get my act together. There's motivation, if I ever heard of it before. My mother and my oldest sister graduated from there. I didn't want to attend an all girls' school. I liked the odds of boys to girls at Mississippi State. When I attended in '67 there were eight boys to every girl. Everywhere you turned there were boys and more boys.

I continued my sports activities while I was at State. I played intramural football, basketball and softball. Matter of fact, after I took all my basic courses, I took physical education courses in hopes of majoring in P.E. and someday being a coach. I was told there was not a major program for girls. I talked the director of athletics into letting me take the courses, and when I went to register I was denied the cards to those classes. I found my brother at the nuclear engineering table, and he went with me to talk to the coach handing out the cards. After much explaining, the coach threw the cards at me. My first day of class shocked me to no end when the coach walked in the room. I said to myself, "Well, here's another F!" to make matters worse, I had told some of my sorority sisters about getting into some of the classes, so they signed up too. I was not the most popular girl in the class. I didn't know till later that I was the first girl to insist on taking P.E. classes. Thank goodness I didn't fail Track and Swimming class. How embarrassing would that have been?

I had a lot of growing up to do in college. I didn't get any support from my dad, emotionally or financially. Mary refused to allow my dad to give me even a penny. I had to ask for help for the last two years, or I was going to have a drop out and work for awhile. My grandparents stepped in and paid for tuition and books, and the rest was on me. There was no way they were going to let me drop out after eight grandchildren had finished ahead of me.

The whole time I was away from home I felt abandoned by my family. Everybody had their own lives to live, and it didn't include me. Occasionally, when my boyfriend would go home, I would ride to West Union, Mississippi, to visit my sister Lou. Mississippi State had turned into a suitcase college, and it was so lonely staying in the dorm over the weekend.

I think what I missed the most in my college years was attending church. Sometimes our sorority would go and sit as a group, but I needed to be involved in Bible study. I wasn't praying on a regular basis. I kept Jesus on a shelf and didn't call on him unless I was in desperate need of something.

When I found out my fiancée was cheating on me and had been for the whole two and a half years that we dated, I was blown away by all the lies and deceptions. Another mad had let me down and couldn't ever be trusted again. I didn't know God was working on another man who would change my life forever. We wouldn't worry nearly as much if we could understand how God is in control 24/7. He never sleeps. But most of all, He doesn't need our help. I have always wanted to fix everything myself. If I had been patient, then maybe I would have had an easier life.

I needed to find a ride to Clarksdale, Mississippi, so I could go register to attend summer school with my sister C.P. at Delta State College. I thought a change for the summer would be just what I needed. How little did I know how much. I called several people I knew from Clarksdale, and none of them were going home on that particular weekend. I called my sister to tell her I couldn't find a ride, and she informed me that she had already found me a ride with Gary Gaines. She instructed me to call him at the freshman dorm. He was out, but a friend of mine that I had gone to junior high with answered the phone and said he would give Gary the message. It wasn't long before Gary called and told me when we would be leaving and made arrangements on where to meet. I waited outside the dorm with my suitcase, and I'll never forget that little blue Falcon pulling in the circle to pick me up. I wondered why they were laughing. I found out later that when they asked my sister what I looked like, she told them I was fat. I wanted to beat her for saying that.

I got in the back seat, and it wasn't long before I was sitting on the edge of my seat. Tailgating has always made me nervous. I feared for my life before we had even gotten out of the city, and we had a two to three hour trip to make it to the delta. Gary and his roommate had a lot of questions, and so did I. I wanted to know how they knew my sister. She had taught them history at Coahoma High School. The weekend went fast, and before I knew it Gary and Doug were back to pick me up for our trip back to Mississippi State. This time Doug was driving, and they insisted I sit up front with them, which made a tight fit. I certainly didn't mind, and I don't think they did either. This was the start of a whirlwind dating period for Gary and me. We were married nine months later.

During the last two years of my college life, I lost Grandma Trussell from Hurricane Camille, and Grandpa Simpson died from St. Palsy. These were two major strengths in my life. Grandpa Simpson wouldn't sit down at the table unless I was by his side. I was the only one he wouldn't let comb or brush his hair and oh, how I loved it! He was the only man I completely trusted, other than Uncle Arnold, of course. Grandpa would let me do just about anything I wanted. He gave me my nickname even before I was born. It's on my baby bracelet that the hospital gave me.

My grandmother was named Vera Beatrice Beck Simpson, and Grandpa didn't like the name Vera so he called her Beattie. When he found out that I was going to be named Vera Catherine Simpson, he immediately decided to nickname me Veedie. So the family called me Veedie, and at school I was called Vera Catherine. It's a southern thing to be called by a double name. I've always been proud of my name because both my aunt and my grandmother have played very important roles in my life, especially after Mother passed away. Till this day Aunt Catherine has always been there for me. She's the only one still living from that generation. I call her often. My trips to Houston are to see her and high school classmates. I also have to drive by the old homestead. I regret having sold the property because

I would love to be able to walk around and sit under that old oak tree where I spent so much time. I spent hundreds of hours in the yard looking for four-leaf clovers. I don't think I expected to have Lady Luck shine on me, but it was a peaceful activity that allowed me to escape from reality for hours at a time.

The other place I spent a lot of time was Mother's gravesite. I guess I felt closer to her there. There was a tree that shaded her grave, and I would sit under it and talk to her. I did more crying than talking. It's been thirty-eight years, and I still cry when I think of her and the horrible death she had to go through. I keep asking God why do such good people have such bad things to happen to them. No where in the Bible does it say if you follow me there will be no trials or tribulations. Matter of fact, He tells us the opposite. He instructs us in Matthew 7:24, "Therefore anyone who hears these words of mine and puts them into practice is like a wise man who built his house on the rock." I hate to think how I would have handled things if I had not had the foundation that God talks about. He knows what's in store for us, and we have no clue what's ahead. I've asked myself hundreds of times how does an unbeliever handle life's tragedies without the Lord. What hope do they have? Nothing from what I see. If I had not known God and Jesus Christ were there beside me, carrying me, comforting me all the days of my life, I couldn't have gotten this far.

To this day I still feel abandoned in a sense. I don't have a lot of friends close by, so I talk on the phone a lot or e-mail someone every day. If it weren't for my dogs, I think I would feel more alone. I guess growing up there were so many people around that I got used to having a lot of people around me. I would love to spend more time with the girls, but they have busy lives. I'll have to wait for grandchildren.

So many people in my life have died and are dying now, and I have always had a problem letting go. To make matters worse, Gary has always said, "When I die, you will need to know how to do this or that." He thinks because his father died early that he will die early. He does have an A-type personality. It used to bother me a lot, but now I'm a stronger person and feel like I could spend the rest of my life alone. I would probably buy more animals. The only drawback is when you want to go out of town, you have to get someone to look after them.

CHAPTER 5

INDEPENDENCE

The only years that I have ever felt that I have been able to make decisions on my own were in college. I didn't always make the best decisions, but does anyone? We are all human, and we all have made mistakes that we wish we could do over. That's part of growing up. If there was really a chance to redo things, I would not have spent eighteen years of my life consumed with grief. This robbed me of so many happy times I could have been spending with my family and friends. I know if Mother could have come back to tell me one thing, it would have been to get on with my life. Time is so short, and there is much to do for the Lord. It's every Christian's responsibility to spread the good news to all the land. Have you ever thought of how happy the very last person saved will be when he finds out he was the very last person allowed in heaven? Talk about getting in by the skin of your teeth! I know I'm not going to be that person.

I have finally come to the realization that Satan does whatever he can to make the lives of Christians so miserable because he is furious that he has lost our souls to Christ. Satan knows he's a defeated foe, and he knows what his future is. My favorite quote is, "When Satan reminds you of your past, remind him of his future." I love it!

As a child I used to watch cartoons and I can remember seeing a child with an angel on one shoulder and the devil on the other shoulder, each trying to get the child to choose their way. When I have negative thoughts today, I imagine that scene. I take my fingers, and I thump the devil right off my shoulder. It gives me such joy to be able to do that. We are the only ones who can control our thoughts. If we would use the power of Jesus' name, we could do so much more. Demons have to flee when Jesus' name is mentioned. Through the power of the Holy Spirit there is so much we can do in His name. I've seen it happen.

God always places special people in our lives, and I have been blessed many times over. I have a dear friend I met through church whom God knew I needed in my life. Mamma Dot didn't have children, so she adopted several of us from the ladies' class. She has been instrumental in my using the anointed oil, which I had never been exposed to before. She has guided me in my walk with the Lord and has shared her life with me. Wisdom certainly comes with age for most people. Notice I said most. There are some who refuse to grow up, like Peter Pan.

I wish I had the knowledge I have now when I was younger, but God has been steadily at work with me. It's great how He never abandons us even though there are times we think we are alone. We are never alone. C.P. has had to remind me over the years to stand on God's promises. I had to go look them up. I couldn't have quoted them to you to save my life. How many of us can quote the Ten Commandments? Not many. I don't know why we don't continue to memorize Bible verses when we are older, but we don't. I have trouble remembering, so I print verses and place them where they can be seen clearly, like on the bathroom mirrors. We all look there several times a day. I have learned the hard way, there's no better way than to depend on the Lord. We can't do things alone. When we can't, He can!

CHAPTER 6

MARRIAGE

As a child I used to daydream of getting married. What little girl doesn't? I dreamed of everything being perfect in every way. I had good solid marriages to go by with my grandparents and my parents for examples. Why wouldn't my marriage be the same? I was swept off my feet, but I had thought before this was the person I would spend the rest of my life with. I was so fickle growing up. I would like one boy one week and another boy the next week. How was I expected to find one person I could spend the rest of my life with? This was so scary to me. What if I made the wrong choice?

Most of my break-ups were because I had decided to end the relationships. My first break-up that was the boyfriend's decision came right after Mother died, and it was a devastating blow. This was the first boy I had really felt was my soulmate. We were so close that I never dreamed we would go our separate ways. How was I supposed to go on with my life after losing two key people in my life in such a short period of time?

Then came my senior year and another steady boyfriend. We broke up in July because he wanted to date other people even though we were going to attend the same college. We dated only two other times, once in college before he headed off to war and once after he came home. The last time I saw Sammy was at the VA Hospital in Memphis, Tennessee, dying from cancer. I set up a scholarship fund for his children because I felt so sorry for them having to grow up without their dad. I had a lot of experience in that department.

Then came the two and a half years of a very destructive relationship. I wasted those years in a dead-end relationship that wasn't good for either of us. It was during this time that God sent my future husband into the picture. I met Gary while Jim and I were still trying to work things out. God made it abundantly clear that I was to end the engagement to Jim.

Gary and I dated almost every night during my last semester at Mississippi State before I headed to West Union to do my practice teaching. We wrote each other letters and talked on the phone a few times but didn't really see each other till I called him during the Christmas holidays and asked him to come to Houston to see me. When we walked in the door, I had this feeling that he was the one I was supposed to spend the rest of my life with. We talked, and I asked him to marry me. Needless to say, there were no plans, so we ran off and got married. Now I understand why there are classes for couples to discuss very important issues before getting married. We had not discussed where we could live, how we would handle the budget, and most of all whether or not he wanted children. There was no doubt in my mind whether I wanted children. I used to say I was going to have five just like Mother. As the years passed my number would shrink.

We started off with ten dollars each and a Gulf credit card in my name. We had to put the hotel room on my gas card. I didn't have a car, so I don't know why I applied for a gas card.

I guess I was hoping someone would buy me one for graduation. Talk about humble beginnings---this was it. Have you ever heard anyone say, "You can't live on love alone?" We found out the hard way. We wouldn't have had rings, but Gary's roommate Doug and his father gave us $100 and Gracie also gave us money.

We lived in a cabin on Uncle Arnold's property because there was no other place to live. We lived rent-free for six months as a gift from my aunt and uncle, which helped a lot. My grandparents stocked the refrigerator and the pantry. I never knew how expensive it was to start out from scratch.

I got a job teaching at my old school on a B certificate because I was lacked four hours to finish my degree. I finished and graduated in January 1972, a whole year after we were married. Gary was still in school, so things were extremely tight. To make matters worse, we had to move into the basement of Dad's house because my aunt and uncle had to rent out the cabin for income. Thank goodness it was for only a year. I couldn't have stayed there another minute.

Finally graduation day came for Gary, and we were moving to Jackson, Mississippi, for his first real job. I couldn't find work in Jackson, so my cousin got me an interview at Copiah Academy. It was located twenty-six miles south of our apartment, which made it easy for me to just get on the interstate and take off.

We were members of Alta Woods Baptist Church, which was not far from our apartment, and we became active in sports for the church. Things were going great while we were in church together but that wouldn't last long.

Then came a big move to New Orleans, Louisiana, which was so far away from family and friends. We made friends, but they were not the kind you attend church with. I noticed Gary was drinking more and more. I didn't need a drink to socialize, but some people do. I guess he was one of those who needed to loosen up first. Problems with his behavior started cropping up. I gave him several warnings but to no avail. I wanted to start our family, and he wanted to continue his good times with his drinking buddies. He had promised me that we would start after six years. Six years rolled around, and he was not ready. He wanted a house first. We lived in an adult community that didn't allow children. I finally had to put my foot down. I was turning twenty-seven, and I was afraid to wait any longer for fear of having an unhealthy child. I wasn't getting any younger.

Years rocked on and the drinking got worse. Most of our fights were over money. I learned it's not the money but control. Gary was a control freak, and he wanted a total control of everything and everybody. He took over buying the groceries because I couldn't stretch the money to buy enough food to feed the family. Several times he gave me the budget to see if I could do any better. There just wasn't enough money to go around. He was having 6 percent drawn off his income before he received his check. How many families can afford to do that?

I was forced to quit my job due to health problems, which added even more stress on the marriage. I became more and more depressed. I started thinking I had made a horrible mistake in choosing Gary for a mate, and there were times I wished Gary would just go away or die. I needed peace at any cost.

Then the physical abuse started, and I had to call in help. There was no way I was going to put myself through this and risk the health of the girls. My sister and her husband came up to talk to Gary. Of course, he lied to them. From this point on, I couldn't trust him.

The headaches grew worse and worse. The pressure from crying just added to the problems. My weight went up due to the stress and the different medications I was on. I was miserable. Thoughts of suicide entered the picture again, but that was not the answer. We weren't in church, and I desperately needed help. I attended a few churches in the Jackson area but didn't feel welcomed. My life was so messed up, and there was no support anywhere for me. Gary and I weren't talking to each other except for fighting. We couldn't agree on anything. At this point, I decided that when the girls were old enough to go off to college then I would leave Gary. This was the only relief I could come up with. He refused to go to counseling.

I would find myself looking for someone else while I was on the road working on research projects. I had already thrown in the towel on this relationship, so I was looking out for myself. I was in credit card debt, and I knew I would have to find someone who could help me get out of debt. Gary sure wasn't going to bail me out. I knew after the divorce I would be left with some of the debt. I can't even begin to tell you how much I've spent on raising the girls over the years. I know it's in excess of $165,000. I knew once Gary found out how much in debt I was, he was going to leave me. He had already said as much. I didn't even know how much debt I was in. I was too scared to add up the totals. When we finally sat down and put the pencil in paper, it was in excess of $42,000. I think I was just as shocked as he was on the amount.

We applied for a mortgage loan to pay off the cards because the interest rates were upwards of 21 percent. I had been paying only the interest charges and still living off the cards. I was waiting for timber cuttings to pay off the loan, but they didn't come even though the contract said there would be cuttings every four to six years. I used the lease payments off the timber to pay the interest on the loan for years. Gary paid part of the interest and some on the principle every year. Then came the day that Gary said he was filing for divorce. It was the Friday before Tiffany's church shower for her wedding. Perfect timing for whom? I was devastated! I was so distraught I ended up in the hospital three weeks before the wedding. This is when the doctors performed the second heart cath. I had fluid built up around the heart and was scheduled to go to have the fluid removed. I can praise God here. He removed the fluid for me without them having a needle to do it. I was able to share that miracle with the staff attending me that day. It was indeed a miracle!

After the wedding, Gary and I started marriage counseling with Dr. Tom Elkin in Memphis, Tennessee. It's been two and a half years, and it's been a rough ride. We're having to rebuild our trust of each other. I thank God for Dr. Elkin. Not only has he helped us put our lives back together, but he has seen us through some rough surgeries. I continue to see Dr. Elkin to help me with life's problems. There's always something going on in my life. I tell people there is never a dull moment! I think I need to thank God for thinking I could handle all these problems with His help. I had considered writing a book before, but Dr. Elkin convinced me that there were people who needed to hear my story. I want it understood that I didn't write this book to harm anyone in any way. This is the life God gave me.

CHAPTER 7

CHILDREN

After a few months of trying and being so disappointed, I finally got pregnant with our first daughter, Heather. It was one of the happiest days of my life to see her so healthy, with all ten toes and ten fingers. I was so relieved. We had a new car, a new house, and a baby in less than two months of each other. These were major changes.

Then came the news we were moving back to Mississippi. That's one thing about the Federal Land Bank---you never knew when you might be told and given two weeks' notice that you were moving. Talk about fruit basket turn over. It always caused a chain of events. In order to climb the corporate ladder, you had to be willing to move wherever they said. This is part of the business world that I don't care for. I had never seen anything like it in my life, and I wasn't sure I wanted to be a part of an organization like that. Like it or not, that was my husband's job.

As we were laying the foundation for our new house, I found out I was pregnant with our second daughter, Tiffany. I continued to work, but there were health problems with Tiffany that made me miss work a lot. After tests at Le Bonheur Hospital in Memphis, we were told that the nervous system was not fully developed and it was hoped she would outgrow the seizures. I was a nervous wreck. I thought I had damaged her when I dropped her at two months old.

I tried to hire help to keep the girls at the house, but I had to let the help go when I came home one day and she was asleep on the couch. Later when Gary asked me who had been in his vodka, I realized that the babysitter had been drinking, having visitors over, and placing long distance charges on our phone. My job was not worth this.

What took a toll on me over the years was trying to raise our family while continuing to work. I was burning the candle at both ends, and the health problems were catching up with me. I was forced to quit work after repeated trips to the emergency room with migraines, strep throat, the flu, and finally pneumonia. To top things off, I was having female problems. I think that was the closest I've come to a complete nervous breakdown. I was put to bed on several medications that made me sleep a lot and gain weight. I felt totally out of control.

Heather was getting sicker and sicker by the day. I think God wanted me home, so I would notice there was a major problem brewing with Heather. We made a midnight run to the emergency room with uncontrolled vomiting, and it was then that the attending woman doctor told me that she thought Heather hated herself. My knees got so weak I could barely hold myself up. Surely this woman who had never seen us before was wrong. What did she see that I didn't? I was the one that was with her 24/7. How could I have missed that?

At the doctor's request, I made an appointment with a clinical psychologist to have her tested. Dr. Baugh sat me down to discuss the test results and in fact, Heather had laid the foundations for an eating disorder. There wasn't much out at that time about the diseases, but I do remember Katie's Secret and Heather's interest in the movie was like none I had ever seen before.

Another trip to the emergency room occurred with a hospital stay of a week with all kinds of tests done. This is when I really became concerned. Things were not going well at work, and there were rumors that the farm credit banks were going bankrupt. Dr. Baugh had offered to help Gary through the bankruptcy, but he refused to go for counseling. Then came the news that the rumors were in fact coming true, so Gary moved into foreclosures, which meant we were moving yet again.

We were all upset over losing the house, having to move, making new friends again, attending new schools, and having to leave the rabbit behind. There wouldn't be room for the dog and the rabbit in a small apartment in Starkville. This was way too much for any one person to have to deal with. No wonder the kids were suffering so. There was, however, a wonderful church and a wonderful preacher who would help us through this transition. Dr. Lloyd baptized the girls in the same water. It was the sweetest moment of my life. To see both girls saved in such a sweet way was enjoyed by all. Thank goodness nobody swam out.

It wasn't long before I was forced to have female surgery, and nine weeks later we were moving again. I begged to stay in Starkville with the girls and let him commute. Gary wouldn't hear of it.

Nobody knew with each move that Heather was growing increasingly more insecure. Dr. Baugh had told me to keep an eye on her. With proper help she should be alright. I saw her getting more and more upset with her changing body. She was so thin but would make comments that she was fat. I knew the disease was progressing. When we moved to Senatobia, Mississippi, there was a boycott in progress. There was a lot of tension in the halls at school. This semester was the final straw that pushed Heather over the edge. She immediately got involved with the wrong crowd and became more and more rebellious. The last week of school I checked her out to go to Batesville, Mississippi, to see Dr. Rayudu for an analysis. We weren't there ten minutes when we were told Heather would have to be hospitalized. We made preparations to admit her to Parkwood Hospital. It took a week to contact the insurance company and make plans. This week was one of the hardest I've ever had to live. There are no words to describe my feelings to you on how much it hurt to admit our child to a mental hospital. To make matters worse, Gary didn't believe it was necessary. He said he thought it was just a phase she was going through and that it would pass with time. I had to force him to agree with me on this one. If he never agreed with me on anything else, Heather's life depended on this decision.

On June 10, 1990, we admitted Heather to Parkwood Hospital, and my heart was breaking. I cried all the way home and spent three days crying my eyes out. I was allowed to call to check on her but not allowed to talk to her. They put her through a series of tests, which is required. We were asked to sign a contract stating that we would not partake of any drugs or alcohol while our daughter was in treatment. I found out later why. During this time God had to carry me because I was so upset that I couldn't even think straight. What if she never came home again? I knew deep down in my heart that she needed professional help but locking her up was so devastating to me. My father was so worried that he made C.P drive him to see me. He wanted to go to the hospital to see Heather, but no outsiders were allowed. Sunday was the only visiting day and then only immediate family members were allowed. I learned a lot from the Dr. John Bradshaw films they made us watch every Sunday before they would let us see Heather. It was a requirement. I'll never forget one comment Dr. Bradshaw made. He said, "Ninety, eight percent of all families are dysfunctional and the other two percent are lying." I firmly believe that everybody has some degree of problems. You can't live in this world and not have problems.

After eight weeks we were finally able to bring Heather home, but we were required to go for counseling for six more weeks. I was warned that if our fighting didn't stop she could relapse, and this time we might be burying her.

Things did not go well. Gary' anger got worse. I refused to allow alcohol to be consumed in the house, and he very loudly objected. He wasn't going to have anyone tell him what he could or could not do. It didn't matter to him who it hurt. Isn't that the way all alcoholics react?

I had my back against the wall, and I had been told what my responsibility was in this matter. I was to protect the children at all costs according to the doctor. I made plans to take the girls back to Starkville till Gary could get his act together. It wasn't a hard decision to make once I was told what would happen to Heather if I didn't make plans to secure a safe place for her. I refused to bury her! I would whatever it took to get her back on the right track. I went to the library and checked out every book I could get my hands on about eating disorders. I went to Al-Anon once a week and took the girls to the teen meetings against their wishes. We were going to survive this. God had proven himself several times to me that He would never give me more that I could handle and things were getting harder and harder to handle. I had to put my whole faith in God's hand and hang on. It was going to be a bumpy ride. It was during this time that I started having flashbacks involving my brother Don.

Gary signed up for counseling with one of the doctors in Memphis who helped treat Heather. He went about three times and then informed me that I was the one with the problems and that I should continue to go without him. Aa you can imagine, this went over like a lead balloon. What had basically happened here was we had been tricked into moving back to Senatobia under the pretense of working things out. It didn't take long to figure that one out. It wasn't long before Tiffany started losing weight, and I feared she had picked up the same bad messages about her eating habits. I made an appointment with Dr. Luscomb as quickly as I could, but I was so relieved to find out she was not obsessed with her body as Heather was. I knew I couldn't handle having two daughters with eating disorders.

Several years passed with monthly sessions and even a few in college were needed to help smooth over the rough edges. We had no idea that someday Heather would get her doctorate in the same field of study. She definitely has had the experience of being there when it comes to eating disorders. This is when you can see God's hands at work. If Heather had not had this problem, would she have been interested in going into this area of work? I believe God uses trials and tribulations to guide us into His plan for our lives. I would never have thought I would be designing Christian material for Emmaus Walks. It's the experiences that God uses to get us where He needs us to be. You do have to be in tune with God to realize these moments. He doesn't just hit you over the head with a 2x4 to get it into your head, although I'm sure at times He would probably like to. I can imagine God sitting there on His throne with His head in His hands, shaking His head at some of the things I've done in the past. Thank goodness He has a lot of patience.

The girls are doing fine. They are married and at the moment they are both living close by. My fear is that when Heather finishes her doctorate, she will move away. I enjoy eating with the girls on a regular basis even though they live very busy lives. I'm looking forward to grandchildren. If you don't believe me, you can come look at the nursery and see all the bears, rabbits, books, videos, games, and clothes in the closet.

CHAPTER 8

LIES AND DECEPTIONS

My father was dying, which added to the already tense situation at home. I was feeling depressed over the bad relationship between us, and it was too late to mend it. My stepsister tried to convince the family that we needed to force Dad to move in with her so she could have complete control of Dad and Mary. Dad vowed he would go into the nursing home before he would ever move in with her. My stepsister went to the nursing home and asked if he would be allowed to stay there on oxygen. Dad was on oxygen because of his emphysema, and they would not accept anyone on oxygen. She already knew that. While my father was in the hospital, my stepsister borrowed their car so she could have the house keys to make a copy of herself. The keys had been changed to keep her from taking things from the house.

I refused to agree with my stepsister on what to do with Dad, so she turned things around on me and told the family that I was the one forcing Dad to be put in the nursing home. I said no such thing. I told the doctor I would take my father into my home before I let my stepsister do anything with my Dad. Unfortunately, Dad believed my stepsister even though he heard me tell the doctor I would never let that happen. Dad was confused at this point about whom he could trust. I didn't go home for a long time because I was dealing with the sexual abuse that had decided to make itself known.

Something happened at the hospital that triggered a very unpleasant memory for me, and I was in the bathroom throwing up and having a panic attack. I had to excuse myself very quickly.

On the way home, I was trying to make sense of the panic attack, but I couldn't put the pieces together just yet. It wasn't until I had a nightmare and woke up crying that it all came flooding back to me. I started throwing up again. I decided at this moment, if I was going to get better, I had to confront my brother. That's what I had learned at my Al-Anon meetings. You have to relive it to get it out and then face it. I called Don at work and I was screaming at him and crying at the same time. He tried to calm me down, so he could make sense of what I was saying. After he realized what I was talking about, he started crying and asking for my forgiveness. It was too early for forgiveness. He promised to do whatever he could to help me through this crisis. He said if I needed to tell the rest of the family he was okay with it. I told everyone but my dying father. Remember I told you in the beginning that Don was Dad's favorite. I could not do that to my father. I wanted to let my father die in peace. Telling my father would not have helped me in any way to recover from this devastating experience. Only my Heavenly Father could help me get over this. It didn't come till years later.

Dad died July 22, 1991. I saw him last on a Wednesday, and he died the following Monday morning with my sister Lou by his side. My last words to him were, "I love you." Lou called a few minutes after he passed to tell me he was gone. When I hung up the phone, I lost it. I cried over all the years of discord and hate that I had experienced. The only peace I had was over the fact that he was not only in heaven with our Lord and savior, but he was reunited with Mother. I wasn't the only one who felt that way. My cousin said on the way back from the gravesite that he imagined Raymond was getting a scolding from Mother for having brought Mary into the family. Mary caused so much pain and suffering. No one was given a break.

I'll never forget the comment my stepsister made at the funeral home while we were waiting to go to the church for the funeral. It was raining and sun shining at the same time, and she said that she had always heard that when it was raining and sun shining at someone's funeral, it meant that that person was going to Hell. I could have said something, but I just said to myself, "I know who's going to Hell, and it's not my father. I had always heard that it meant the devil was beating his wife. I don't know who makes up these things but this one was ludicrous. I have to ask myself what was her purpose in saying such a hateful thing to us. What had we ever done to her to deserve such a comment?

I would have only one more contact with my stepsister. I went to see Mary to see if she would let me buy the baseball seats that belonged to Dad. My dad had verbally promised those seats to me. My stepsister did all the talking. My stepsister didn't go to college, but she was an Ole Miss fan for some reasons. I guess because we were all Mississippi State fans. She wasn't using the tickets. She was giving them away to people in town so we couldn't have them---another way to inflict pain on us. I could not bear to go to the baseball stadium and see someone else sitting in my father's box seats so none of us attended any games for at least two years.

Before the meeting was over I asked where my Mother's cedar chest and concert violin where. I was told they were still in the storage building on our property. Knowing full well I would drive out to the place to look for Mother's prized possessions. I don't know how they thought they would get away with that lie. Lord knows they told so many. I had Uncle John Hugh, my father's brother, with me because I knew how they made up so many lies that I took him along for a material witness. They would have told some wild tale I'm sure. They probably would have said I forced my way into the house and threatened them in some kind of way. That was their style. I wasn't going to give them anything they could use against me. Well, you can only imagine how I felt when I opened the storage building to see everything had been removed. I found out later that my stepsister had Mother's cedar chest at her house. It was there when I was present. My stepsister outright lied, with the chest sitting in the next room from where we were sitting. The violin was taken to the dump on Highway 15 north of town. How much trouble would it have been to pick up the phone and call one of us to come get Mother's things? I was called months after Dad died but to drive all that way and then I was told nothing. When I arrived, Mary was throwing up and didn't say two words to me. She was the one who called me and said to come get something she wanted me to have that was my father's. I left with nothing. I found out later from the maid that Mary had been told that she was going to move in with my stepsister or she would not be back to take care of her.

I remember the last time I spoke to Mary she was complaining that my dad had not left her enough money to live off of. I informed her that he had left her a lot of insurance money. I asked what had happened to it. I didn't get an answer, but I got a look from my stepsister that could kill. I noticed that my stepsister had new floors, new cabinets, and a new van. Where did those items come from? I would bet my last dollar that the insurance money purchased those items. I knew my stepsister didn't make that kind of money at the health department.

I ran an ad in the Times Post asking if anyone had found Mother's violin at the dump on Highway 15. I have seen people digging in dumpsters, and I was hoping someone had pulled the violin from the trash. It wasn't worth anything to anyone except the family. I had played with it as a child, and I wanted it. I got one call from a former dance student of Mother's that said she remembered Mother bringing it to class and playing it for them. She had noticed another ad in the paper stating that someone had found a violin on Highway 8. I read that ad, and it belonged to a musician who had stopped to change a flat and the violin had fallen off the trailer. I helped the musician get his violin back. No such luck on Mother's violin. It was gone forever.

Mary's health continued to fail and my sisters visited several times but not in the presence of my stepsister. C.P. told Mary that she would turn over Mother's cedar chest along with a smaller chest that belonged to her. Mary was told that we would not be back to visit her unless she did the right thing by turning over Mother's property. When my stepsister returned from a trip to Texas, she became enraged by the visit from my sisters and word was sent to them that if they put their foot on her property again they would be arrested.

Mary had a stroke and ended up in the hospital, and she asked that C.P. be called to come see her. My stepsister called, and C.P. declined. My stepsister was told she had to hand over the two chests first. My stepsister brought the two chests to C.P.'s mother-in-law's house and dump the chest on the driveway. Mrs. Winters opened the door and told my stepsister to bring the chests into the house, which she did. Mrs. Winters called C.P. and told her about the delivery. C.P. called me and told me she wasn't sure from the description Mrs. Winters gave if they were in fact Mother's chests or not, but I needed to go to Houston and check it out. Gary and I made the long trip, and sure enough they were Mother's chests. They were in bad shape, but we put them in the truck and headed home. I cried all the way home. What an ordeal I had been through to get a pile of cedar. But it wasn't just cedar to me. This was all I had of Mother's possessions. You would have thought it was a chest filled with gold. It meant the world to me to have something that was once Mother's. How would Mary's family have felt if we have taken something of their mother's and held it hostage from them? They would have had us arrested, I guess.

Here lay the main difference between my family and Mary's. We had been raised with values and morals and taught the difference between what's right and what's wrong. We were taught to respect other people's property and never to take what's not ours. I can remember Mother telling us never to hate anyone. This is what Mary taught me. I didn't hate anyone till she moved in and took over. Satan had a run for his money with Mary. I don't which one has been the meanest to me. They both were an evil force to be reckoned with. The similarities don't stop there. Mary would lay up in the bed and read from the Bible and pretend to be a child of God, but I saw through her deception. I'm not sure if people in town or at church saw through her or not, but they told me on many occasions that she was nothing like Mother, to which I quickly agreed. It didn't take a rocket scientist to figure that out.

Mary always pretended to know a great deal about nothing. You could put in a thimble what she knew. I remember once we got into it at the hospital when someone mentioned that I looked a lot like my mother, which always rubbed Mary the wrong way. Mary said that I might look like my mother, but that my father made my whole insides. I asked her to explain that statement, to which she had no medical reason because there was none. I marched back to the lab and had a friend type my blood. I didn't know what blood type I had, but my siblings had A negative. My father was O positive. My mother didn't even know she had A negative blood until she was typed for surgery. Sure enough, I was A negative with one component being positive, which I had explained to me later during some testing means that I am A positive. I pushed the report in her face and walked off. This one time Mary was speechless! The reason Mary didn't know a lot about medicine is because she didn't go to school beyond a high school education. A doctor she had worked for trained her. That was it. So Mary never knew anything more than the doctor that trained her. There's a dangerous situation. I could go on here and tell you things that would raise the hair on your arm about things I saw and heard her do, but there would be no point in boring you.

I asked a friend of mine if he would repair the big chest. He said he would be honored to. He was so upset over the story he refused to take any money from me. He said I had been through enough just to recover the prized chest. I can't tell you the joy I felt when I went to pick up the chest. Sam had made new feet, put in a new bottom, and made a new scroll for the back. The chest had been restored to its former beauty. Till this day I have Mother's chest in my bedroom where I can enjoy and look at it every day.

I have only told you a few of the many nightmares my family and I have endured from my stepmother and her daughter. The years have taken a toll on my health. I knew to get better I had to be able to forgive. This was an impossible task for me, but with God's help I knew that someday I would finally be able to be free from this bondage. I felt Mary's hand reaching out from the grave, strangling me like in the end of the movie Carrie. Now there is a scary scene! The poison that she had inflicted on me was growing inside of me

When I left that last day I saw Mary, I arrived home and destroyed every picture she was in. I got rid of anything she had given me, which wasn't much. I gave to charity the thin quilt she had given me when I went off to college, and the only other gift I had was a large print Bible that she and Dad had given us when Gary and I got married. I ripped out the page she signed and gave the Bible to Hope Ministries for some poor family to enjoy. I don't think Mary and Dad purchased the Bible. Why would we need a very large print Bible when I was twenty-one and Gary was twenty? How many young couples need a large print book? I don't know of any. I figured the Bible had been given to them.

This proves to me that Mary would not allow my father to spend any money on me. My father paid for the flowers and the pictures for Lou's wedding, just a few years ahead of mine. Mary complained about it for years. My sister saved her own money to pay for everything else. I was so impressed with my sister's talent in pulling off such a beautiful wedding for such little money. I made a promise to myself that day that whatever kind of wedding I had, it would not include Mary. I would not have Mary sitting where my Mother should have been. I would not allow Mary to ruin my wedding day no matter what. That's why Gary and I ran off and got married. I knew I would have to pay for everything, and I didn't have the money and I didn't want to start off in debt. I had been in four weddings, and Gary had been in five, and we decided that was enough for us. We thought it was a waste of money.

There's no way I can list all the lies and deceptions that I endured. The book would weigh so much you would have trouble lifting it. There is one that has surfaced recently that I didn't know about until it was brought up during a conversation with my brother Don. Don said Dad asked him a few months before he died what he had done to me. Don thought I had told Dad about the abuse, which I had not. I asked Don what he said to Dad. He said he basically denied everything. This enraged me to no end because I had been so careful not to tell anyone that would tell him, and then he lied to my father, making him think I was the one lying. I told Don that Dad was in heaven, and he knows the truth now. It wasn't until a few days later that I finally realized that when Dad was in the hospital and Don spent a week with him was before I got my memory back about the abuse. Dad was talking about why I didn't want to come to Houston to see Don while he was in town. He wanted to know what was going on between us. I felt much better after I realized that no one had actually told Dad about the abuse, to my knowledge.

I have finally forgiven Mary and my stepsister, which was a very difficult task for me. The Lord lifted my burden and rid me of my poison. I'm still working on Don's forgiveness. It's hard to forgive someone when they refuse to admit to the family what they have done. Don is still lying to others. I realize he needs a great deal of help. My prayer is that Don will repent and ask God to break his bondage and go for help. I would love to be able to see and hear Don some day give his witness to help others who are in bondage. I want my brother back. God can change anyone. There's proof of that in the Bible!

CHAPTER 9

HEALTH PROBLEMS

It wasn't long till we started having a lot of problems. We both came into the marriage with a great deal of baggage. I think it was the first month that I realized that the birth control pills had to go. My headaches were getting worse, and I gained twenty pounds the first month. I got off the pills and tried and IUD but had to have it removed after two months. We began to fight over the least little things. But the fight over my smoking was a major issue. I had tried over a two-year period to quit, but I had picked it back up the summer I attended Delta State. I was told the cigarettes had to go or he would. Talk about an ultimatum! One month of marriage, and I had to decide between cigarettes and my husband. I threw the cigarettes away, but every time we had a fight I would go buy a pack. I would smoke a few, and then I would throw them away. This became very expensive for a young couple who barely could make ends meet.

Next came the threat that he was leaving if I didn't get control of my depression over the loss of Mother. I admit the grief consumed me, but I didn't know how to deal with it. I needed professional help. He walked out one night, and I didn't know if he was coming back. I went in the bathroom and found a razor and tried unsuccessfully to cut not one but both of my wrists. I was so upset! I'm not sure what stopped me. I guess I was afraid that it was an unforgivable sin, and I didn't want to take that chance of not making it to heaven. Nothing mattered more to me than getting to heaven. I had to be able to be in eternity with my Lord and Mother. If I did nothing else, this had to be accomplished.

I tried other types of birth control pills, mainly to help get control of my periods. I had an extremely small uterus, and it would contract like the beginning of labor every month. I ended up in the hospital many times due to the massive pain and finally due to the allergic reaction to the hormones. I found out that I had too much estrogen in my system, and the pills were overloading it to the point of vomiting, which led to dehydration. I remember an intern telling me once when he couldn't stick my vein that I needed to be written up in a medical journal because he had never heard of a person who was allergic to birth control pills. After he stuck me for the fourth time I told him to go get the doctor or he was going to be asking for assistance to remove the syringe from a place he couldn't reach. I was in no mood to be abused by an intern. If it had been up to me he would have been kicked out of medical school for talking to a patient that way.

I had such a rough time monthly, I considered asking a doctor to perform a hysterectomy on me, but I wanted to have children more than anything. I loved children, and I had to have them at all costs. I wish my husband had been as anxious as I was. I remember getting the news that I was pregnant while I was at work. My husband was dropped off by the car pool so he could pick up our car, and I took my supper break and met him in the parking lot to tell him the good news. He walked off from me and mumbled, "I hope you're happy. You finally got what you wanted." He drove off, leaving me there in the parking lot crying. I made my way back to the employee lounge and cried until it was time to be back at my station.

I didn't find out that I was pregnant until I had completed training and had worked one week for Masion Blanche. I worked till I was eight months pregnant. I spent a lot of time throwing up because I was forced to wait till one or two o'clock to eat when someone would arrive to take over my station. I wasn't allowed to even sit down until the head guy came by one day and felt sorry for me and ordered a stool to be placed behind the counter. I would not have worked as long I did, but I was told I had to pay for my clothes, the doctor, and what the insurance did not pay for the baby. From that moment on, I was forced to pay for all my clothes and the girls' clothes. Gary had me over the old proverbial barrel, and I complied.

My next hurdle was when Tiffany was born, and Gary insisted that I have my tubes tied while I was on the table. I wanted more children, and he didn't. Guess who won that battle? I thought since he didn't want any more children that he should have surgery. That went over real well. I wanted to be able to have more children if something happened to him. I might be able to have more with someone else should I remarry. The argument was that I was going to already have my deductible, and he would have to pay to have something done to him. I was told if I didn't have the surgery that he would not touch me when I got home. Well that's a fine "how do you do!" I wouldn't need surgery if that were the way it would be, now would I? I should have stood my ground because over the years I have held a grudge against him for making me have surgery.

Five years after the tubal ligation, I started having some serious female problems. I was forced into an early hysterectomy due to tumors that caused excessive bleeding. The headaches got better for a while, but then I noticed one day while taking a nap that I couldn't see the numbers on the clock just a few feet away from me. I had opened only the left eye, and everything was so blurry. I closed the left eye and opened the right eye, and things were clearer. I called and made an appointment to see an eye doctor, and all he told me was there was some damage to the optic nerve and that I needed to see a specialist.

Well, we were moving again in a few weeks so I made an appointment to see a doctor in Oxford at the same clinic where my family had been going for years. In fact, Dr. Rayner had operated on the girls when they were babies. Heather had tear-duct surgery twice and Tiffany had lazy-eye muscle surgery. I couldn't see Dr. Rayner, who was my choice, but he was not seeing regular patients anymore. He did cataract surgeries and cornea transplants. He operated on Lou's eyes when she went legally blind, so I knew he was the best. I had to settle for Dr. Supple. I was told there was damage to the optic nerve again, but nobody had a clue why. It was the right eye that I had splashed Liquid Plumber in when we lived in New Orleans. I almost lost my eye, but it was due to a quick response that saved it. After three months, I was told that I had made a complete recovery, which was a miracle. If I had known then what I know now, it would have been a piece of cake. I guess God was preparing me for the worst. I had watched my sister Lou go legally blind, and it was heart wrenching. She had two surgeries to correct the problem, but she is left with damage due to a prescription being read wrong or filled wrong. Never in my wildest dreams did I think for even a moment there was a chance I might lose my sight.

    I continued to see local eye doctors, but no one knew what was going on. I should have been referred to a specialist in Memphis, Tennessee. It wasn't until I started having trouble keeping my balance that I thought there must be something wrong with me. I had my mind on all my food allergies and trying to keep my migraines under control. Then came the trip to New York. I wasn't feeling well so I went to see Dr. Ruhl for a sinus cocktail. I thought this would make me feel better. Wrong! I noticed every time I got on and off the elevators that I got real dizzy. We were in a hurry to get dressed and get something to eat, and we rushed right out the door so we wouldn't be late for the play. We arrived five minutes before the show was to start, so I ran into the bathroom. I entered the room just as they were lowering the lights. I couldn't see a thing! It's a good thing we had an usher, or I wouldn't have been able to find our seats. In case, you're wondering, we saw Miss Saigon.

Returning to our room, I noticed in the mirror that my left eye was swollen. I asked Gary what he thought, and he said it looked swollen to him. I brushed it off and went to bed. Sunday was our day to sightsee. We had a full day planned, so we got off to an early start. We had breakfast in a deli under the World Trade Center. I took a picture outside of the towers, and I got dizzy just looking through the camera. I almost fell I was so dizzy. Then it was on to Central Park, and we walked more than I would have liked but that's the only way you can really get a closer look. We were in and out of the stores, and finally we took a break for lunch in the Trump Plaza. I asked if we could take a cab back to the hotel. I was not feeling well. We took a short nap. Then came the NBC tour, and it wasn't until we centered the "Saturday Night Live" studio that I suddenly got real dizzy and had to sit down. The nausea hit me, and I tried to decide if I could go on with the tour. The chest pains started and didn't last long so we continued the tour. We stopped on the way back to the hotel and grabbed a bite to eat at a deli. We shared a sandwich since we had already made plans to eat at the top of the World Trade Center at the Windows of the World Restaurant.

We took another rest and then began dressing for the night, and I was feeling much better. Things started going wrong in the elevator to the top of the World Trade Center. I suddenly got so dizzy that I had to hold on to Gary or I was going to fall out on the floor. Severe nausea swept over me, and my chest started tightening up. I thought once we got off the elevator it would stop. We entered the restaurant, and I walked over to the window to see the view and started swaying. I immediately stepped away from the window. I first thought I had eaten something that had made me sick, but why wasn't Gary sick? I went over in my mind the whole day, trying to figure out what could be making me so sick.

Then the drinks arrived. I took one sip, and it was like an explosion went off in my chest. I couldn't speak. Gary was asking me what was wrong, and I couldn't talk. It was scaring me, and he was getting more and more concerned. Gary ordered dinner, but I couldn't eat. The waiter noticed that there was something wrong and asked if he needed to call 911. I shook my head no. I was so sick I couldn't even get out of my seat to go to the ladies' room. The waiter checked us out as soon as possible and as we were leaving the restaurant I got sick at my stomach again, so I ducked into the bathroom. I spent several minutes there, but I didn't throw up. As I came out of the bathroom, I noticed that the elevator was broken down. We had to wait for a man to come and escort us down while one was being worked on. I got sick in the elevator again and almost fell on the floor again. Gary sat me in the lobby of the Marriott while he went into the mall to find a drugstore. He bought several products, but none of them worked. I tried all of them before the night was over. I felt like a gorilla was sitting on my chest all night long.

It was the Fourth of July, and there was a ton of things planned for the day, so we started early with breakfast on the New Jersey side. We took the subway over, and I was feeling much better. We watched the flyover and the fleet of ships. It was all impressive, but I think what I liked the most was all the security. The Blackhawk helicopters and the Navy Seals were my favorites. We headed back to the hotel to eat lunch and take a nap to wait for the fireworks at Battery Park. It was beautiful but crowded. I don't like crowds. I was glad when it was over so we could head back to the room.

The next morning Gary left early, going to a meeting on the New Jersey side. I didn't have a clue where he was going. I got up later and walked over to the financial district a bought myself a cappuccino. I sat outside for a few minutes watching people hurrying to their offices. I walked over to the Hudson River to watch the ferry crossing the river. I noticed the waves were real rough. Suddenly the chest pains started and the nausea set in. I was standing there thinking, Here I am alone in New York with only my room key and some change in my pocket. I asked God to please let me at least make it back to the hotel so they could figure out from my room key who I was if I passed out or died.

I walked slowly back to the hotel. I made it up to my room and called the secretary at the church to tell her to find me a replacement for vacation Bible school for the following week. Glenda begged me to call downstairs and at least tell the front desk that I was sick. I was afraid they would insist that 911 be called. I promised to rest till Gary got back from his meeting. Gary arrived and I didn't have time to tell him what had happened during the day. He said we had to get dressed to meet a group downstairs in thirty minutes. We were going on a dinner cruise on the Hudson River. So off we went. I was excited about the boat cruise because I have loved boats all my life.

From the moment we stepped on the boat, I could not stand alone. Gary had to escort me everywhere, even to the ladies' room. I had to hold on to everything I could get my hands on. Talk about a strange situation. I got a chair and parked myself. After supper I took a pill for allergies and felt better. Everybody was headed outside to see Lady Liberty. I made my way out the door and held onto the rail for dear life. We had some friends make some pictures for us. There she was, in all her splendor! A close up view of Lady Liberty was definitely a highlight of the trip. If I died right here on the spot it was well worth it!

My last day in New York was not going to spent in our room, so off I went to Soho for two hours by myself. I wanted to buy a few Christmas presents, and I had to have a Yankee baseball hat. I've followed the Yankees since I was a child. I used to watch games with my dad. That's one thing we've had in common over the years, baseball games. I can't believe I did that by myself, but when you think you maybe dying you do things you wouldn't normally do. I hope I get back to New York someday.

When the heart problems started I became very concerned about what was happening to my body. My father had told me on many occasions that Simpsons had good hearts. Then why was I having dizzy spells and chest pains? After two heart caths, I was told I had a section of my heart that appeared to be damaged from a virus. This was news to me. I racked my brain trying to figure out what virus. I did have strep throat several times that I had let go too far and ended up in the E.R. Maybe this was it. It wasn't until I was in the delta on an assignment that I realized something was wrong with my motor skills. I suddenly couldn't fill out my time sheets and expense report, and I couldn't see to read without my glasses. I would catch myself getting closer and closer to my reading materials. I told my advisor to call in some help to finish the project because I was going to have to go in the hospital for some tests. I knew something was terribly wrong with me.

I contacted my regular doctor, who by the way was a sixth grade student of mine from years ago. He ordered some tests, and in a six-week period I was told I had osteoporosis, diverticulosis, small nerve damage to my left hip, carpal tunnel syndrome in my wrists and ankles, a damaged heart, rheumatoid arthritis, and a tumor behind my left eye. I can't even pronounce the name of the tumor, much less spell it. Did I think my world was falling apart? Literally. I was coming apart at the seams!

The doctor who saw me at Semmes Murphy didn't think my experience in New York seemed unusual, but he noticed my left eye wouldn't go up or out when I was told to follow his finger. He sent me straight to Methodist South Hospital to have a MRI of my head. I didn't think too much about the MRI because I've had so many in my lifetime that to me this was just another test. What I did notice was how the staff treated me. I had been there before, and I wasn't treated this nice before.

The MRI was a long one. It took almost two hours to complete the test, and I had to wait and bring the film back with me, which is something I've never had to do before. It was obvious to me that this was a different test from the ordinary MRIs I had had in the past. While I was waiting the nurses were extremely kind to me, even asking if they could get me a coke. I've never had anyone ask if they could get me a drink before. I thought to myself, I must be dying! Finally the films were ready to go, and I headed home. I was too scared to look at the film. What was I suppose to be looking for if I did get up the nerve? Beats me.

I waited till the next day for an afternoon appointment with the same doctor that had ordered the test. I gave the receptionist my films and took a seat. There wasn't another soul in the office, and I heard the doctor tell the receptionist to get a surgeon on the phone because the patient had a tumor and would require surgery. I wondered whom the doctor was talking about because I was the only one in the place. A few minutes later I was called into the doctor's office. I noticed he was checking out my mental well-being because he asked how I was feeling today. I said, "Fine." He sat there a minute trying to decide how he was going to tell me the bad news. The pause was so obvious! It screamed volumes to me. The doctor said he had good news and bad news. Which one did I want first? I said I wanted to hear the good news first. The doctor said that I didn't have a brain tumor like he thought I had. Deep down I knew that's what he had thought because of the urgency with which he ordered the MRI and my having to be back the next day with films in hand. I had worked for doctors enough to know there was something going on, and it had to be serious with all the symptoms I was having.

I braced myself for the bad news. The doctor said I had a tumor behind my left eye that would require immediate surgery. I asked a few questions, but he said it was so rare that he was referring me to Dr. Jon Robertson, who knew more about this particular kind of tumor. From that moment on, he didn't answer any more of my questions. I made the remark that our daughter was getting married in eight months and that I couldn't have surgery till after the wedding. The doctor said that the wedding might have to be postponed until after the surgery. This comment really worried me. Just how serious was this tumor? Was I going to die? All kinds of things raced through my mind. Did Mother have cancer when she was carrying me and was this related in any way? On the way home, I wished I had not driven myself to the doctor's office alone, but then again, I didn't really expect bad news. I convinced myself I couldn't drive the thirty-some-odd miles to my house without hurting others or myself, and God delivered me home safely.

Now came the task of telling my husband the bad news. He never liked hearing about any sickness of any kind. He suffered in silence with his shoulder pain, and he didn't want to hear about anyone else's pain. I didn't want to break the bad news, but it had to be done. He was in as much shock as I was about the tumor. Nobody in my family had ever had tumors that I knew about except Mother's cancer. This is what bothered me the most.

It took about two weeks to get in to see Dr. Robertson. He took a skeleton of the skull and showed us exactly where the tumor was located and explained how the tumor would be removed. We had a lot of questions, but first he wanted me to see Dr. Fleming, who would explain more about the tumor. This was the first time I had been told I would lose my eyesight forever in the left eye. It was a devastating blow! I tried not to cry in front of Dr. Robertson, but when I got in the car I broke down. Gary tried to be consoling, but it wasn't helping me any. He wasn't the one losing an eye. I called the girls from the car phone because they were waiting to hear what the doctor had to say. It was very difficult to talk. I told them it wasn't good news and that I had to see another doctor before anything would have to be done. I just wanted to get off the phone as quickly as possible. I wanted to be left alone. I spent a lot of time in bed over the next few days trying to get a grip with the news. I would cover up my left eye to see just how limiting it would be for me. It didn't seem that bad, or was I fooling myself?

We waited about another two weeks to get in to see Dr. Fleming. His office was packed, and it took awhile to get in to see him. I couldn't help but notice all the patients in the waiting room. Most of them had big patches over at least one eye. I sat there and stared at them, wondering if any of them had the same tumor I did. I didn't find out how rare my tumor was till we talked to Dr. Fleming. When we looked at the films for the first time, there were several interns present because Dr. Fleming wanted them to see this rare tumor. I was told this tumor was so rare that there were only four surgeries in Memphis a year involving this type of tumor. I was told it was not hereditary, which was a relief. I certainly didn't want to pass anything like that on to the girls. I have passed on a few of my allergies but so far nothing serious.

Dr. Fleming was very matter-of-fact with his explanation of things and left us alone in a waiting area to think about what we wanted to do. I wanted to have surgery immediately, but Dr. Fleming suggested a biopsy first. We needed to know if this tumor was cancerous or not. Most of these are not, but there is always a possibility they can be, especially with the family history.

The biopsy was scheduled for the day after Thanksgiving, which was about three weeks away. I feared the surgery would have to be canceled when I got sick on Thanksgiving Day and vomited all through the night. We were checked in at the hospital very early in the morning and with my nerves and unsettled stomach I was not in the best of spirits. The surgery didn't last long, and I was in my room by midday. I throw up every time I have surgery, so you can imagine how great I looked. My eye started swelling badly, and the bruising got worse as time went by. Gary and my sister Lou kept me supplied with ice packs, but the swelling didn't respond at all. My head was busting. Finally I was released to go home on Sunday.

Monday morning I received a call from Parkwood Hospital where Heather was working. They informed me that Heather had been in a bad car wreck and that there were ambulances on the scene for transport. I asked them to keep me informed as to where they would be carrying our daughter so we could be getting ready to head in that direction. I called Gary at work first so he could be headed home to pick me up. Next I tried to reach Andy, Heather's husband, at work, and he had not arrived yet but was on his way there. I asked them to tell him Heather had been in a wreck and wait there for information in case she would be brought downtown, where he was. Next, I called Andy's father, John Hardison, at work and he said he was nearby, so he said he would go to the scene and see if he could get any information. When John arrived, Heather was still in the car. The techs were working on getting the other victim in the ambulance because she was in the worst shape, with a possible broken neck.

John talked to Heather and found out she had refused treatment and was a little confused as to what happened. The tech told Heather if she had not had her seatbelt on, she would have been thrown through the windshield and would not have survived the accident. After seeing the condition of Heather's car, John thought it was best if she was checked out at the nearest hospital. We were called and told to go to Germantown Methodist Hospital. We were already on the interstate so we had a good twenty minutes to reach the hospital from where we were. Thank goodness, Heather only had some bruises and abrasions from the seatbelt and the airbag. The car was a total loss.

When Heather was describing the accident she said the woman turned across her path as she was going through the intersection. The air was knocked out of her, and she said everything went white with the airbag going off, and she couldn't breathe. Then there was this strange male voice speaking, and she wasn't sure where it was coming from or who it was. A type of the Left Behind series had been left in the tape deck, and the accident slammed it into the tape deck making it play. We got a good laugh about that one. It was what the woman in the other car said she experienced that gave me a chill up my spine. She said as the van was turning over she felt a presence holding her in the seat, like an angel. She ended up with a broken vertebra in her neck and some broken ribs but very lucky to be alive.

My biopsy was very unimportant compared to the wreck. My view of everything changed when I feared our daughter's life was in danger. All I could do was praise God that Heather had been spared and was in good shape.

Waiting for the test results of the biopsy was not easy. You can't hold your breathe that long. I kept asking God to give me the strength I needed to hear the results. I had already been told a ton of things that were wrong with me, and all in a six-week period. How much more could I take? I had long talks with God about this not giving me more than I could handle statement. I told God he was meeting his quota real quick on this one. I didn't know how much more I could take, but God did. It's not fair that He knows the beginning to the end and we don't. Then again do we really want to know what's coming? I can't tell you how many times I've begged God to come and get us.

This growing old business has never been a favorite thing of mine. I always told my father that I would rather die young than to grow old and have to have someone feed me or have to bathe me. I watched my grandparents go down and it's not fun to watch loved ones get so feeble. My father said I just wanted to be a good-looking corpse. My response was, "You've got that right."

The biopsy came back negative, and we were told now I t would be a waiting game. We had to wait till my eyesight got to a certain point to justify going in and removing the tumor because once it was removed, there would be no more sight. I had a problem with that. My fear was the doctors would wait too long and the tumor would grow out into the brain area and that's where the optic nerves join. If that happened, I would go totally blind. I didn't want to risk that, but the doctors insisted they knew what they were doing. I couldn't understand why it wasn't my decision to make.

I went for regular office visits and field tests to determine how much sight I was losing, and it seemed like all I was doing was having doctor appointments one right after another. I was getting sick of constantly going to Memphis for doctor visits. I'm not a very patient person. I guess I'm best described as one who wanted it yesterday. I think that's a fair assessment of me. I tried to keep busy planning a wedding to take my mind off the impending surgery. There was only so much I could do with that. Then 9/11 hit, and I was glued to the television stations 'round the clock. I had gotten up early that morning, and as I was letting the dogs out, I happened to turn on the television, which I didn't normally do that early in the morning. There on the news was an account of what they thought had hit the World Trade Center. I stood in front of the television set in shock. We had just been there the year before for Opt-Sail and stayed at the Marriott attached to the towers. I remembered a conversation I had had with my husband when I found out where we were going to stay. I asked Gary if that wasn't where the terrorist had bombed the towers. I had watched it on the news but couldn't remember much of the details. He said, "What's the chances it will happen again?" I guess it's like people thinking lightning doesn't strike twice in the same place, but it has and it does.

When I saw the second plane approaching the second tower, I couldn't believe my eyes! My brain kept thinking, This is not happening. It's not real. It was so horrible it was beyond words. Then the towers collapsed, and all I could do was cry and pray. I kept seeing the faces of all the people I had talked with in the stores in the mall beneath the towers and remembering the people in restaurant that had waited on us. It was a nightmare. Then I remembered giving my brother information on where we stayed while we were in New York because he was going to be moving from a power plant in New Jersey to one in New York. I gasped for air when I realized that I might have sent my brother into harm's way. It took me seven hours to find out where he was and if he was okay. Thank god he was north of New York City. I couldn't help but notice the flight plan of the plane that was supposed to fly to Washington. The turn it made looked like it turned right over the area where my brother was working at Weswego. This plane later crashed in Pennsylvania.

Several days later I learned that a sorority sister of mine had lost her husband in the collapse of one of the towers. He worked for the Port Authority and stayed with the building while others were trying to get out. Several of my sisters made the trip for the funeral, but I wasn't able to go. The whole experience of just watching the people on the television looking for their loved ones upset me to no end. That was the saddest thing I think I have ever watched on the television. It stirred up a lot of emotions for me.

Two days later I headed to Grenada Lake to work an Emmaus Walk and when we arrived, part of the lake was closed due to the threat of the dams being blown up. I never thought about the dams. I think 9/11 opened a lot of people's eyes to just how safe are we in our own communities. New York is a long way away, but then we saw all kinds of precautions being taken right before our eyes. I guess living in a small southern town we don't think about big city problems. Life is a lot slower here, and I'm thankful for that.

The biopsy was negative, and I was thankful for that. I spent a lot of time in and out of the doctor's office for more tests. Finally came the day to remove the tumor. I was sent to Methodist Central for a MRI that would tell the doctors exactly where the tumor was and how big it was so they would know where to go in. I was not happy with the way they were going in, but I didn't have a say-so in the matter. It was explained to me that they would make an incision from ear to ear about an inch into the hairline. This way the scar would not show up. Then they would pull down my face and drill a hole into the skull. They would remove the top part of the eye socket and remove the tumor. The eye socket broke, and they had to shave some bone off my skull to replace the piece they broke. I told my surgeon that I wanted him to take a close look at my brain and of course he asked why. I had always heard that every time you learn something new, you get a new wrinkle in your brain. I wanted to know if I had a lot of wrinkles or was my brain smooth. He thought I would forget about that comment, but after I came out of ICU, that was the first question I asked him. He laughed at me and told me I was very smart.

The surgery was around eight hours long, and I was in ICU for three and a half days. I remember the pain and vomiting. My IV leaked into my arm and caused a lot of problems. The poor boy who had to change it was rattled because he had trouble with my rolling veins. I assured him it was not his fault. He kept apologizing. I explained to him it was me.

The vomiting was getting to me. The doctor had said that the vomiting would be damaging to the surgery. It causes a lot of pressure in they eyes. I was getting very depressed and was crying more and more. I heard one of the nurses say if she could figure out by the clock when to give me my shot that maybe she could keep me from vomiting. I was thinking that shouldn't be hard to figure out. I was too doped up to help her. There was no way I was going to be released to my room as long as I was throwing up. This is when I asked God to allow me to feel all the prayers that I knew people were lifting up to the Lord for me. There was a sudden warmth that surrounded me. I felt like Jesus had laid down on that bed and put His arms around me. I drifted off into a sweet sleep and when I woke up the nurse was wheeling me to my room. There were tons of flowers in my room. This made me feel even better. But what pleased me the most was to be able to see my family.

My sister and my first cousin had driven to Memphis to see me. I didn't remember talking much to them, but they were there for me. I remember wanting to wash my hair real bad but I couldn't sit up in bed without getting real dizzy. It was days before I was allowed to wash my hair. I answered the phone a few times and shocked the callers. I don't remember what I said but I hope it was nice.

I had to learn to walk with a walker for a few days till I could get my balance. There were major adjustments ahead of me. I was glad to be home. I had a lot of company at first. Everybody didn't want to see the hundred-plus staples in my head. It was a horrible sight! A few staples got overlooked and Gary tried to remove them with a staple remover and pulled a few stitches loose. I had to call my friend Teresa who is a nurse to come and remove them for me. That was a bad experience. Never let your husband try to remove anything!

My cocker spaniel, Maddie, was extremely glad to have me home. By this time my oldest sister C.P. and Bill had arrived to spend a few days with me. There wasn't much people could do for me. I wasn't in the mood to eat so I slept a lot. Maddie is a mommy's girl, so she curled up with me on the couch. I wasn't able to lay flat, so I had to try and sleep propped up on the pillows. Now I was on my own. I had to try and learn how to get to the bathroom and bathe without any assistance. It was a long road to recovery. I wasn't able to drive for weeks. It would have been months, but I practiced with a patch leading up to the surgery. I'm glad I did. I couldn't see me stranded for months at the house. I was back at church in two weeks, and people almost fainted when they saw me. People were calling me Job. I didn't like this because I'm not a man. This is when I came up with the name Jobulene. I would tell them to call me Jobulene instead. I would get the strangest looks, but I think they understood what I was saying.

One of my friends kept asking me how I was holding up to all the bad news and it kept coming. There hasn't been much of a break for me but what was I suppose to do? Was I suppose to lay down and die? You have to deal with the cards that are dealt. We aren't able to pass the problems on to someone else or ask God to take them back. I steadily asked God to give me the strength to put one foot in front of the other. I lost friends to cancer during this time, and I counted myself blessed. Dr. Elkin asked me if I was angry with God, and he was surprised when I said no. I told him there were so many who were far worse off than me. How could I be mad at God? I was still living. I told Dr. Elkin that I was angry with God for a very long time for taking my mother away from me, and I made up my mind I would never do that again. God knows what's best for me, and I trust Him to follow through with His plan for me. Whatever that plan is, it must be mighty for me to have to go through such horrible things. I've become a very strong person because of the trials. I like to call them tests. I don't like to fail tests!

The health problems are still on going. I've had more surgeries and will have more in the future. At the moment, I'm being watched for a detached retina in my one and only eye. I still have a problem with itching on my scalp from nerve damage, and I'm being fitted for an ocular prosthesis. The shape of my left eye is changing, and the pressure has dropped. The prosthesis will help hold the shape of the eye and will give me an appearance of normalcy. My major concern at the moment is my spine. There is nothing between the two bottom vertebra in my lower back, and the sciatic nerve is giving me fits. I feel another surgery on the horizon.

CHAPTER 10

BACK AGAINST THE WALL

I've learned when you think you have your back against the wall, there's always someone else who has things even worse than you. I know at times you think your problem is the worst, but really deep down you know that's not true. I think Satan wants you to think that.

I watched the war in Iraq from my couch, and I heard the horrible stories of torture and murder. Here we have had a free life. Those people know all about suffering. No peace whatsoever! Neither have the people in Israel or Palestine or other third world countries had the peace we've had here in the United States. I think that peace is now gone, now that terrorists have brought their battle here on our soil. We will forever be looking over shoulder for the next attack. I don't spend my time worrying about it, though. Who holds my future? God does. This is why God wrote the 23rd Psalm. God knew the dark times that would be ahead of us and that we would need the comfort of His words to go with us. I quote that verse often.

I've been in the shadows, and my life has been in danger, and God has been every step of the way with me. I learned that Psalm as a child, and I still use it as an adult. We are to keep our eyes focused on Jesus and not to be distracted from it. If you think of yourself on a high wire with Jesus on the other end, then keep your eyes on Him and don't look down. It's while we are distracted that Satan tries to sneak in and catch us off-guard. He's a clever old devil. I bet he's pulled every trick in the book and then some. If he would try to tempt Jesus standing on the top of a mountain, what do you think he will do with you? Everything possible. Don't leave the house without your shield of protection. When our girls would leave going to school, and they were driving, I would pray for them all the way to school. I had to pray especially hard when Tiffany was driving to Memphis, Tennessee. It's hard enough when they are older but Tiffany was fifteen. Memphis traffic is hard enough for adults. It's dangerous!

Someday when we get to heaven I think God will allow us to see the dangers that were around us. I think it will be interesting. You may not think so. I've always been interested in what cannot be seen by our eyes. I think that's why I'm so interested in angels. I have collected them over the years. They are all around me.

CHAPTER 11

PRAYERS TO GOD

If I had to list all the prayers I've prayed to God, there would not be enough paper in this world. He gave us the Lord's Prayer to use as a guide. I used to wear it around my neck as a child. I had a cross that in the center was a tiny opening that revealed the Lord's Prayer. I would try my best to read it whenever I would sit still enough. I was always on the move.

I got to pray at the supper table on a few occasions. I loved my grandfather's prayer. It was short and sweet, and I was always hungry. I said my prayers at bedtime, too. I'll never forget the prayer I said one night that I wished for the mumps, so I could stay home from school. Well, I got my wish. My sister kept reminding me to be careful for what I prayed for in the future. That's true. Sometimes we ask God for things that we don't know are bad for us. That's why it's so important that we let God make those decisions. Remember, He knows the bigger picture.

I pray for so many people that I had to start a journal to keep up with my prayers. I post the date, name, reason for prayer, and date of the results. It amazes me how some of the prayers turn out. It's important to see that God does answer prayer. That's why I post the results. It may not be the answer you want, but God does answer your prayers.

I believe that Jesus and the loved ones who have gone before us are in heaven praying for us. They know we need it. Why wouldn't they be praying for us? Prayer is our direct line to God, and it's open twenty-four-hours a day and night. While we are asleep, they are awake and praying. That is comforting to me.

At our church we have hedge prayer for the pastor while he is preaching, and I think that is so awesome. We also have a group that prays with Brother Gene Horton before he heads into the sanctuary every Sunday. We also have a prayer team that comes to the church to pray specific prayers that have been requested. There is also a prayer chain of people who call to ask for prayers, and then there are e-mails that go out asking for specific prayers for whomever needs it. As busy as we are today, we have to use every form of request we can. I use the Upper Room and the staff at CBN for additional prayers. I also use all my Emmaus friends, who are mighty prayer warriors! I leave nothing unturned. God gave us prayer as a call for help, and I'm going to use it all the time. To me there is nothing so small that we can't go to our Father in prayer about it. I think some people don't want to bother God, thinking he's too busy for their problems. There is nothing more further from the truth. Satan would like for you to think God is too busy for you. Don't buy that lie!

I spent the first hour of wakening talking to the Lord before ever putting my foot on the floor. At night, I spend my last hour awake talking to my Lord. We must humble ourselves, ask for forgiveness, and praise Him. That's the formula for me. I would recommend it for anyone. That's not all the praying I do. I pray at all hours even while driving. With my eyes open, of course. Sometimes I feel a special need to pray without an explanation. It's God calling me to pray. I have found out later why.

CHAPTER 12

CHARITY

Charity was taught to me by my mother's love for others. I think we have to lead by example. I don't think we were born to care about others. I had a lot of things passed down to me, so I guess that's where it started with me. I watched my mother give away clothes and food to those who didn't have as much as we did. I remember Mother asking people from church or school if they wanted to come pick vegetables for sale to the grocery stores in town, so I was happy to see people come and pick what was left. I don't know why I was chosen to call around town to see who needed vegetables, but that was my job. I would report to the garden and tell Mother and my sister Lou how many baskets we needed to fill the orders. Then I had to join in the group to get that quota filled on top of what we needed to pick for ourselves. We then delivered the orders and returned home to shell and can or freeze our food. At least while we were shelling, we got to watch television. We would have races to make the shelling go by faster. I won a few of those races. It was always close.

I have to tell you about my sister's friend, Diane. We were going to teach her how to shell peas. She didn't know what she was supposed to keep and what she was supposed to throw away. I thought she was kidding. I have to say I think people who grow up on farms learn a lot more than city people do. We are exposed to more, I guess.

We never had much in the way of money, but I never considered us poor like some. We pretty much grew whatever we needed. We had the dairy cows and cattle for beef. We grew all our fruits and vegetables. Mom made our clothes until we were old enough to make our own. I wish you could have seen the pea-picking dresses Mom made for us. The material came from the flour sacks. We would wear them over our shorts so we could gather up the hems of the dresses to hold the peas till we got to the end of the row to dump the peas into the baskets. This allowed us to work really quickly. You didn't have to drag the basket with you. I wish I could say that was my idea, but I'm sure it was Mom's.

With both our parents working, it was still hard to make ends meet with five children and two adults to feed. I wish I had a video of us eating at that huge table my father made so we could all gather around the table all at one time. Things went fast. You had to get what you wanted on the first pass. Remember the song, "Pass the Biscuits Please?"

After Mother passed away, I carried my old clothes to the Health Department to be given away to needy families. I guess that's where Mother's clothes went.

The sorority I joined at college did charity work for the Palmer House in Columbus, Mississippi. We cooked for the children and gave them presents at Christmas. I was thrilled to see Heather collect clothes and toys for the Palmer House when she was elected Miss Hospitality for Senatobia and Tate County in 1994-1996. Heather later collected clothes, toys, and shoes for orphans in Russia. Tiffany joined a sorority, and they gave the children at the Palmer House presents at Christmas also. It's great when you can see your children follow in your footsteps.

I went on to help out children in the delta when I had a chance. While I was working with the schools, I would give them books, videos, and books on tape for their libraries. On occasion, I would give the schools musical instruments. I gave some children bikes, while I bought others underwear and shoes. Whatever I knew they needed, I had to provide. The teachers helped me in finding out what was needed. I even bought groceries for some. God always placed these things on my heart so how could I not respond?

In the Bible it instructs us to give whatever we have two of away. Keep one and give the other way. When I think of all the clothes we have I feel so bad. Mother always said I had more clothes than the law allowed. I was beginning to think there really was a law that banned the amount of clothes a person could own. I was so relieved to find out that was not true.

Every time I get some timber money, I give to the Mercy Corps for food kits or buy sheep for some small villages. I know each person can make a difference, however small. Instead of buying flowers for funerals I give gifts that honor that person. I would rather give a gift that keeps on giving. I believe charity begins at home.

We have missionary friends we also support. It's not always possible for us to travel to foreign countries, so we support Chris and Kelley Lett in Mexico. It's hard to be away from home and loved ones, so we offer prayers for protection and money for support.

Another way I contribute money is through CBN every month. I have a draft on my account, so the money comes right off the top before I spend any of the monthly money on myself. I love watching CBN and seeing how my money is spent. The children are so happy to receive the gifts, and the surgeries that are provided are awesome. The stories are great! I love being a part of the CBN group. Someday I want to go with a group to give food or toys to children.

Once I am able to travel, I would like to go with Living Waters to South America to help run water to the homes of the very needy people in those small villages where there are birds and other dirty stuff in the only water hole in the villages. I can't imagine how horrible it would be to have to drink that water. Some people have to walk for hours to get water.

If you know of anyone who needs their self-esteem raised, get them involved in charity. It gives a person self-worth. It helped our girls realize how blessed they are and helped them see how the other half of the world lives. It really opens one's eyes.

The most important thing I've learned about charity is, it's what Jesus wants us to do. We are to become more Christ like, and this is the closest we will ever be like Him. He instructs us to help the poor and the needy. My desire is to have a heart like Jesus. Leave a legacy!

CHAPTER 13

COMING OUT OF THE STORM

When Jesus was asleep on the boat, do you remember how upset the disciples were? They thought they were going to drown. They must not have realized who Jesus really was or how powerful He was. They must have thought he was an ordinary man like them but smarter. I would have liked to have seen their faces when Jesus stretched out His arms and told the storm to be quiet. It had to have been an awesome experience to behold. I can just see me hanging on to the edge of the boat with the water splashing me in the face. I know my heart would have been pounding ninety to nothing. I've never been out on the water in a storm, but I can imagine how scary that would have been for me. My husband went deep-sea fishing, and they got caught in a storm about eighty miles out with ten to twelve foot swells. I would have been on the bottom of the boat screaming, crying, and praying for sure. I want to be in sight of land when I go fishing.

I've had storms in my life that have rocked me, and sometimes I've felt capsized. These storms can leave you just as helpless as the disciples felt that night. But Jesus has always been my lifeline. I've even felt like I was going down for the third time, but there was Jesus' hand reaching out to me to pull me to safety. He has always been my beacon of light in the darkness. Jesus is asking us to be His light to the world. He wants others to see Him through us. How hard is that?

We should be jumping for joy to be able to represent Him. He could have chosen someone else, but He's asking you and me to do His work through the power of the Holy Spirit. There is so much power in Jesus' name. We just have to learn how to use it to His glory. Do you know the song, "They Will Know We Are Christians"? The song says they will know we are Christians by our love. There are some people who claim to be Christians, but you couldn't prove it by their actions. Actions always speak louder than words. If you were on trial for being a Christian, would there be enough evidence to convict you?

If you watch real Christians in a crisis, you will see and hear their true beliefs. I've seen proof of this on TV. There's always some reporter sticking a microphone in front of someone who has just suffered a real loss. I can't help but feel sorry for these people. Mother always said, "Don't cry over burnt toast, because someday you may come home and your house has burned down." That's the same as, "Don't sweat the small stuff." Trust me there will be plenty of "big" stuff in your lifetime. You can't wait till it happens. You need to be preparing for it now. Jesus tells us to build a strong foundation because it's not if, but when life's storms come your way.

I'm here to say that I have experienced many tragedies in my short fifty-four years, and I would be foolish to think nothing else will harm me. My battles aren't over by any means. Why should Christians have it easy? Did Jesus have an easy time while He was here?

CHAPTER 14

LESSONS LEARNED

If someone asked me what the greatest lesson I've learned so far in life, it would have to be that I am worthy. Through Jesus Christ I am made worthy. Nothing I've done has made me worthy. I haven't made any major contributions or accomplished any great feats. Satan has tried his best to make me think that I'm not important or that my opinion doesn't matter. I know differently. I am a child of God, and there is nothing anyone can do to change that.

Another lesson I've learned is that you have to walk the walk and talk the talk. What good is your witness if someone sees you doing something wrong or hears you talking about another person in an unflattering way? I told my girls that there were always little eyes watching them at school. If you are doing things just to get your name and picture in the paper, then you need to question your motives. God states that such things will be burned up in heaven.

I've learned that not all good intentions are received well by everyone. Some backfire on you, but you have to carry one. You can't let one bad experience stop you from doing good for others. You dust yourself off and carry on in Jesus' name. You can't make everyone happy all the time. Never do something for others expecting something in return. If you're going to do something, do it because you felt God's calling. How can you go wrong with God's guidance?

Don't repeat mistakes. If you continue to do the same thing over and over then you'll get the same results. You have to change what you're doing to get different results. We intend to work ourselves into ruts. For some reason, we don't like change. This is where I'm different from most. I was raised to be different, not to follow the crowd. I was told to learn something new every day. This mindset makes you look for the different. I have a journal in which I record new facts. I get my facts from all kinds of media. I guess that's why I love CNN so much. It gives the most current and up-to-date news. It brings the world right into your living room.

I've learned never to criticize someone for their actions or make fun of them for the way they dress. This is something I used to do, but the good Lord has reformed me. He used my girls to correct my behavior. To have your own children correct you is a mighty powerful way to get your attention.

I've learned to concentrate on myself and not spend time trying to fix others. If you are busy working on yourself, then you won't have time to find faults with others. God does, however, instruct us to point out to other Christians if they are doing something wrong that will mislead others. There are tactful ways to do this. You don't want to hit them between the eyes with a sledge hammer.

I believe you can learn something from every experience. If you don't learn from it, then you will likely repeat it. I don't like to do the same thing twice.

CHAPTER 15

PLANTING SEEDS

I haven't always been pleased with every place we've lived in, but I believe God sends us where He needs us. I think that's why God put the story about Jonah in the Bible. We can choose to bloom where we are planted, or we can choose to be dormant. I believe God places special people in our paths that inspire, encourage, and grow with us in our spiritual walk with Him. Every church has its pew warmers, and I wonder what causes Christians to sit by idly while there is work to be done. We have about twenty-five people in our church who do everything. We have 400-plus on the rolls. Some have moved and didn't leave forwarding addresses, and some come only on holidays. I think every church has this problem.

I've introduced several really good projects or mission ideas only to be rejected by the members of our church, so I understand why some sit and keep their mouths shut. I work on projects as the Lord leads me. One of my gifts is the encouragement cards. I know firsthand how a card can lift one's spirits, especially if one is down or sick. I've been there. I feel compassion for others, so I have to write notes. God has given this gift to me so I have to use it. Remember what God says about not using your talents?

I also send greeting cards for birthdays and anniversaries. This is not limited to just church members. I also mail get-well cards to people in the community. Cards are a wonderful way to let people know you're thinking about them. In the fall it's especially important to send the freshmen from our church cards to let them know that even though they may be out of sight that we haven't forgotten about them. I want them to know that I will be praying for their safety and protection from evil while they are away from home.

I try to plant seeds everywhere I go, even hospitals. I have witnessed to people in the operating rooms while I was preparing to have surgery. I would prefer not to have so many surgeries, but if that's where God needs me, then I'll go. My husband was praying with me before my last surgery, and the nurse asked him if he was a preacher. She said he sounded like a preacher. I told her he has had a lot of practice praying with all my surgeries. You never know who's listening.

My most valuable planting to date is the one with my friend's daughter, Amanda Williams. I've adopted Amanda from a very early age and have encouraged her over the years. Amanda has a very loving spirit and I can see God using her to inspire others. I'm on her to-call list at school, if she needs to check out early. Amanda helps me out around the house, and she fills a very important void in my life since my girls are grown and married. We write each other encouragement cards all the time. Amanda introduces me to her friends as her grandmother, but I keep reminding her that I'm too young for that. I'm really her second mother. Amanda is a gift from God!

I wish we had a mentor program in our church, but the closest thing to that is to sponsor a child in the confirmation class. Members sign up to participate.

I believe Satan uses our busy lives and confusion to steal time away from us so we can't spend more time with our Lord. That's why it's so important to set aside quiet time for meditation, prayer and reading. You can't have spiritual growth without these three things.

CHAPTER 16

MAKING YOURSELF AVAILABLE

Making yourself available is extremely important if you're going to work for the Lord. If you are burdened with a hectic work schedule or have a very large family to care for, you will miss many opportunities if you aren't looking for them. I've learned over the years to listen to people, and they will tell you what they need. If you're doing all the talking, then you can't hear their needs. Also be aware at all times that there are people everywhere that you can touch with a kind word or maybe even a smile. I also give away a lot of hugs a day. A person needs at least 5 hugs a day.

I've had people ask me at wedding showers, receptions, and while shopping what happened to my eye. Children are the most curios. I was waiting in line to get into a wedding reception when a boy around the age of ten inquired about my eye. He seemed very concerned to see an adult with a pirate patch on. I used to play with one as a child, and here I'm wearing one again as a fifty-four-year-old. I told him I lost my eye to a tumor. The look on his face said it all. When I told him that I was born with it, his face got even more concerned. I guess that was all he needed to know, so he ran off and got involved in the activities of the day. I don't mind telling others.

God gave me this tumor even before I was born, so He knew I would use it to tell others about Jesus.

Another encounter occurred at Fred's Dollar Store in Coldwater, Mississippi. As I entered the store a man blurted out, "What happened to your eye?" I explained my story, and he was very concerned about my well-being. He said he didn't know how he would handled such a crisis. I quoted the verse, "And we know that all things work together for good to them that love the Lord." Romans 8:28 has been a long time favorite for my family. He agreed and walked out the door. I could see that the other people in the store weren't happy for the man's intrusive manner. I just gave them a smile to let them know I was fine with the opportunity to share Jesus. I jump at every opportunity I get. I didn't use to share with strangers, but now I feel the urgency of time running out. Who knows how much time a person has in this life? That man could have been killed as soon as he walked out of the store. If I'm the last person to speak to someone, I pray that God gives me the opportunity to share His love with them.

CHAPTER 17

WHY AM I HERE?

Why am I here? This is a question I have asked myself thousands of times. I think everyone has asked themselves that question at some point in their lives. Why are any of us here? We are here for fellowship with God. I have to laugh at some of the things I've done and wondered if God thought that was entertaining enough for Him. It doesn't seem possible that's why we are here, does it? God doesn't need us to do anything for Him. He can do everything by himself. He needs and wants us to fellowship with Him. Now there's something I can do well! I love to fellowship.

One of my favorite past-times is to work Emmaus Walks. That's the greatest form of fellowshipping with brothers and sisters in Christ that I know of here on earth. I see it as getting a head start on heaven. In heaven we'll be fellowshipping with God, Jesus, loved ones, family, sisters and brothers. Why wait till we get to heaven? Let's fellowship now. Let's praise God and sing worship songs now. We have eternity now, whether you know it or not. You will go one place or the other. Which place will you spend eternity? Smoking or non-smoking? When I see people complaining about the heat or the fact that their electricity is off, I have to wonder why they are not concerned about the heat where they are headed. If they think it's hot here, they had better think again.

If God has allowed me to go through all my trials and tribulations so I could write this book, then it's been worth every minute of pain and suffering. If this book helps save one life, then it's been worth it. I want to do whatever it takes to get people to accept Christ as their Lord and Savior. If you are not saved, I want to invite you to ask Jesus into your heart. Accept Jesus, believe Jesus died on the cross for your sins, and ask Jesus to forgive you for your sins. It's that simple. Let Jesus change your life forever. If you are already saved, I'll see you on the other side! De Colores!

www.ingramcontent.com/pod-product-compliance
Lightning Source LLC
Chambersburg PA
CBHW020309010526
44107CB00001B/36